Lessons in Success From the NBA's Top Players

Mike "Stinger" Glenn

Mike "Stinger" Glenn

Cover art by William Tolliver
Book design and graphics by Gerard Munajj

1st edition
1st printing April 1997

1 2 3

ISBN: 0-9649795-5-1

Published in the United States of America
By Michael T. Glenn
As an imprint of Visions 3000 Publishing Co.
1295 G Brockett Road
Clarkston, Georgia 30021
Phone: (770) 496-0420
Fax: (770) 496-1140

Mike "Stinger" Glenn, 1984

INTRODUCTION

My mom, Annye, and dad, Charles, were both teachers. Therefore, education was very important in our household. Mom always told me that as long as I was an honor student, I could practice basketball anytime. This was a great deal and we both kept our ends of the bargain. She would take me to practices anywhere at anytime. As great as the support she gave me, she had an even bigger impact on me in another area. She encouraged me to read books about successful people. When I finished, we discussed the reasons for their successes and the lessons that I'd learned. Her complete confidence in me made me try harder. She would constantly say, "I know you can do it" or "I know you won't be afraid." I tried and am still trying to live up to her expectations. I never want to let her down.

Mom taught me for three years — in the third, fourth and fifth grades — at E.S. Brown Elementary School in Cave Spring, Georgia. Annye Glenn taught school 35 years, completing her teaching career at Coosa Elementary School in Rome, Georgia. She instilled in me the drive to always be my best. She challenged me with questions like, "Can you give me a better answer?" and "Can you dig a little deeper?"

In her classroom, we recited the words of successful people. Her favorite quote to me was "Do not go where the path may lead you; instead go where there is no path and leave a trail."

Dad also offered me lots of inspiration. He always said I could do anything I wanted to do because, as he put it, "Old man *Can't* died a long time ago." In addition to being a mathematics teacher at the Georgia School for the Deaf, my dad was a volunteer basketball coach for 18 years. His deaf students and athletes adopted me into their culture. They taught me basketball and sign language. I spent countless after-school hours and weekends on their campus. From them, I learned that language is merely a medium through which we communicate. It is not a test of intelligence or character. They also taught me that compassion requires more sharing than it does giving. Now for the past 17 years I've conducted a free basketball camp for hearing-impaired athletes. I don't do it to pay a debt, but to continue sharing the lives and experiences of these special athletes.

By the time I was 16, I had learned many lessons and believed I had a pretty good idea of who I was. That's about the time I got one of the biggest compliments of my life. My high school basketball coach, Bob Brannon, and his wife, Mary Anne, named their only son after me and my friend and teammate Jim "Bo" Bragg. They named their son Michael Jim Brannon. I never knew exactly how to thank them, but I sure was proud of their decision. I often think about that very important honor. Through Bob and Mary Anne Brannon, I learned about the motivation and power of compliments.

While playing for National Basketball Association teams, I was amazed at the different concentration and preparation levels of players and teams. I wondered what separated players and teams of comparable talent. Prior to 1985, I wondered why everyone thought Sidney Moncrief was such a good player. He was very good at every aspect of the game, but he wasn't an exceptional shooter or ball handler. He did not have blinding speed. After playing with him in Milwaukee, I now think he was the greatest player that I ever called a teammate. And I've played with some outstanding athletes. All-time greats like Bob McAdoo, Spencer Haywood, Earl Monroe, Dominique Wilkins and Dan Roundfield were all sensational. But Moncrief's total concentration, attention to detail, and focus were greater than I'd ever seen. He could remember how we defended out-of-bounds plays from two months earlier and what went wrong with a particular technique. He knew each player's habits, strengths and weaknesses. He ate proper foods, strengthened his body throughout the season, and believed he could do things that his body, at 6'4" and 185 pounds, didn't seem big enough to do. He seemed to be able to bring all his energy and efforts together on the court. He focused so well that he rarely made mistakes and made all the key moves to win countless games. One season he was able to lead the division-winning Bucks in defensive rebounds, scoring, free throws, assists and minutes played. When I asked him how he could accomplish so much, he said, "I'm not as talented as a lot of players, so I have to work harder." He was a good example of how your mental approach determines your success.

There are lessons to be learned from press conferences, interviews, locker-room conversations, and player appearances. But I find it unfortunate that the public is usually only shown the outrageous, the controversial, or the emotional highlights. I hope this book will be an incentive for the reader to dig a little deeper for a better understanding of how and why these players are successful.

To gather some formulas for success, I asked NBA players to tell me the most important lessons that they had learned about being successful in basketball and in life. I guess it's only fair that I answer the questions first.

In basketball, I think you should practice your shot until you believe that your next shot is always going in. It should not matter if you've missed 10 in a row or made 10 in a row. You've got to believe that the next one goes in the basket.

Also in basketball — and life — I think the most precious treasure is the journey. Once you leave the game what you'll miss most are the experiences that you shared with friends. The awards, recognition and winning are often overrated. Winning is important mostly because your experiences in a winning effort are more fun. There are more smiles in practice, happier people around you and you feel more comfortable and secure. Kareem Abdul-Jabbar had this to say about Magic Johnson; "Magic made us realize that we were having fun."

As for life, I think it is a test of your ability to remain positive and happy.

It includes preparing for the storm. You've got to be prayed up and saved up. Of course you must be strong mentally, physically and emotionally.

My son, Michael Justin Glenn, was only 2 when he summed up the philosophy of many NBA greats with a simple observation. "Daddy," he said, "God wants us to be nice."

Recently, I was part of a ceremony with one of the most respected players of all times. "Dr. J," Julius Erving, was the featured speaker. I may have been more anxious than the attending crowd to hear his message. He presented a formula for success he had adopted and later gave me permission to include it in this book.

"In order to be successful, you need to have the FAT philosophy," he said. F stands for faithful — having faith in yourself and a higher spiritual power. The A stands for available. That means being in attendance when information is given out or taught. The T stands for teachable. He told the young people there that no matter how good they were in their endeavors, they would never reach their highest level of success if they were not teachable.

May all who read these pages remain FAT.

WHAT IS SUCCESS?

To laugh often and much;
To win the respect of intelligent people and the
affection of children;
To earn the appreciation of honest critics and
endure the betrayal of false friends;
To appreciate beauty;
To find the best in others;
To leave the world a bit better, whether by a
healthy child, a garden patch or a redeemed
social condition;
To know even one life has breathed easier because
you have lived;
That is to have succeeded.

— Ralph Waldo Emerson

ACKNOWLEDGMENTS

This book is dedicated to my family. Thanks to my wife, Rhonda, for her support, encouragement, ideas and assistance. I appreciate the inspiration provided by my son, Michael Justin. His presence and his hugs are motivation enough for me to give my best. I especially thank my mom, Annye, and my dad, Charles, for their guidance. Thanks to my older brother, Chuck, for helping me to develop athletically by spending time with me and sharing his friends. My sister, Teresa, a history teacher at Spelman College, Morris Brown College and Clark Atlanta University, has always given me historical perspectives and implications. I appreciate the guidance given b N.A.K. Mutota. Thanks also to Cie Cie Wilson, my editor, Beverly German, and my copy editor Phyllis Perry for their dedicated work and input, and of course the NBA, its players, their public relations directors and NBA Entertainment. Many thanks to one of my favorite artists, William Tolliver, for creating the artwork for the cover of this book.

Michael T. Glenn

CONTENTS

ABOUT THE AUTHOR

Mike Glenn is a basketball analyst for CNN and the Atlanta Hawks. He had a nine-year career in the NBA, where his specialty was shooting. His expert shooting earned him the nickname "Stinger," Mike received the prestigious Walter B. Kennedy Citizenship Award from the NBA in 1981. He established the Mike Glenn Basketball Camp for the hearing-impaired and has run a free camp for 17 years.

Grateful acknowledgement is made to the following authors, editors, athletes and publishers. Their materials were vital sources and resources.

SELECT BIBLIOGRAPHY

Anderson, Peggy *Great Quotes From Great Leaders*

Ashe, Arthur *Days of Grace*

Bell, Janet Cheatham *Famous Black Quotations*

Fitzhenry, Robert *The Harper Book of Quotations*

Gardner, John *Wit & Wisdom*

Gibran, Kahlil *The Prophet*

Great Quotations, Inc. *Quotes From Black Americans*

Hill, Grant *Change the Game*

Hurston, Zora Neale *Dust Tracks On a Road*

King, Martin Luther Jr. *A Testament of Hope*

Kirshnamurti *Think On These Things*

Mays, Benjamin E. *Born to Rebel*

Montaigne *The Complete Essays of Montaigne*

Olajuwon, Hakeem *Living the Dream*

Riley, Dorothy Winbush *My Soul Looks Back 'Less I Forget*

Smith, Sam *Second Coming The Strange Odyssey of Michael Jordan*

Thomas, Arthur *Like It Is*

Thurman, Howard *Meditations of the Heart*

Young, Andrew *A Way Out of No Way*

LET ME EXPLAIN...

On every NBA team there is a dominant personality who leads and sets the example. When that team plays, it assumes the characteristics and style of its leader. Rarely does this leadership come from a coach. Players respond to the coach in the manner that the dominant player accepts his guidance. Even Red Auerbach, legendary coach of the Celtics, needed Bill Russell to co-sign his philosophies.

Each team also has a care-giver. This player listens well, relates to everyone and has compassion. He is always popular because everyone can talk to him. The care-giver is the heart of the team. Much like the center of a wheel, all of the spokes are connected to him.

Even though the team belongs to the player with the dominant personality, the care-giver has great influence and respect. Let me give you a couple of examples

In Seattle, the team belongs to Gary Payton. He dictates the style of play and decides who'll get the ball. He even led the team to support Coach George Karl when support for him was waning. Nate McMillan is the care-giver. He has been there longer than any other player. Everyone on the Supersonics respects him. He can tell one of his teammates to play harder or make other adjustments and they will go along with his plan. Sometimes such direction and scrutiny would not be well-received from a head coach. Both the dominant player and the care-giver are important to the team and in some cases, one player assumes both roles.

Of course the Chicago Bulls is Michael Jordan's team. Michael is the dominant personality who challenges his teammates to play hard and continue to improve. He leads by words as well as example. He demands excellence and the Bulls deliver!

Scottie Pippen is the care-giver. He is more approachable

and less intimidating. If anyone on the team has a problem or a question, they feel they can go to Scottie for help.

Steve Kerr explains, "Scottie is one of the best teammates I've ever had. Everyone loves him. He's so unselfish and plays so hard. He knows where you'll be and when you want the ball for a shot. And he'll consciously try to get you shots. He'll be aware when you're struggling. He cares about everyone like no star I've ever played with."

In the following chapters, I point out the dominant personality and the care-giver on each team and my thoughts about the team as whole. My comments will vary from present players to former players and even to the house band.

The top players on each team share the lessons they have learned from successful basketball careers and successful lives, in that order. Also, I've added some borrowed wisdom from an array of well-known and successful people. These comments may relate to the NBA athletes, the entire team or perhaps just to the reader.

Enjoy!

Scottie Pippen

ATLANTA HAWKS

IN MOST AFRICAN cultures, dance is an integral part of self-expression. There is no distinction between spiritual and recreational dance. Zaire native Dikembe Mutombo brings all of himself to the game. One referee warned Dikembe of taunting his opponents after a blocked shot. The official said, "Dikembe, don't say anything, just play the game." Dikembe responded in his deep, resonant voice, "I can't just play my game. I have to *do* my game." A wag of his finger after he blocks a shot is Dikembe's way of saying, "This lane is the house of Mutombo and I'm the only one who has a key."

Dikembe speaks nine languages and is an international spokesperson for CARE. He also has adopted four children.

"Deek," as he is affectionately called, is the first player in NBA history to lead the league in blocked shots for three straight years.

Once writer and actress Maya Angelou was asked how she saw herself. Did she fit more in the writing school of Paul Lawrence Dunbar, Alice Walker, James Baldwin or Richard Wright? Ms. Angelou answered, "in 1513 Machiavelli wrote 'The Prince,' a slim volume that has become the basis for all foreign, internal and colonial power."

She continued, "The greatest thing he did out of it all is to create one phrase and the phrase is more powerful, more lethal than the hydrogen bomb. The phrase is 'separate and rule, divide and conquer.'"

The prolific Ms. Angelou concluded by saying, "I will not be divided from Baldwin, or from Wright, or from Paul Laurence Dunbar or Alice Walker — none of it. I belong to everybody."

I don't know whether Ms. Angelou follows

basketball, but if she does, she would probably admire Dikembe Mutombo.

Steve Smith, the multi-talented Hawks guard, defines himself as a shooting guard with point guard skills. He seems more comfortable being an agreeable part of a team than a dominating scorer. He plays with the ease and finesse of his childhood idol, George Gervin. But the influence of his late mom impacts his style of play more than the influence of his idol.

Smith says his home was like the community center and his mom, Mrs. Clara Bell Smith, included the neighborhood kids in everything. She is the root of his care-giving character. In a tribute to his late mother, Smith donated $2.5 million to his alma mater, Michigan State University, to build the Clara Bell Smith Student Academic Center.

Steve said of his mom, "She is the inspiration behind the gift. I've had great role models, but none greater than my mom. You can never give too much; I consider this her gift to education, given through me." Mrs. Smith died of cancer in 1992.

Coach Lenny Wilkens leads the Hawks the same way he did as a player. The former point guard wants everyone to contribute. His teams are never dominated by a single player.

Throughout my career, Wilkens was the coach that everyone wanted to lead their team. His respectful attitude and controlled disposition have always been admired. Wilkens was the only person to be named to both the top 50 players in NBA history and the top 10 coaches, an honor he received in 1997 to mark the 50th anniversary of the NBA.

But I find it more outstanding the he was named Cleveland's Catholic Man of the Year. His spirituality keeps him grounded. After the game, you can barely tell the difference between a loss and a win. For the record, Wilkens also has more

"We are all of us deeply involved in the throes of our own weaknesses and strengths, expressed often in the profoundest conflicts within our own souls. The only hope for surcease, the only possibility of stability for the person is to establish an Island of Peace within one's own soul."

— *Reverend Dr. Howard Thurman*

wins than any coach in NBA history.

NBA teams have good trainers, but none better than Joe O'Toole. O'Toole has not missed a
game in 28 years and is involved in most aspects
of basketball operations. His most important
asset is his willingness to help. He'll go above
and beyond the call of duty at anytime. I call him
"everybody's main man."

Dikembe Mutombo

*"Satisfaction lies in
the effort, not in the
attainment. Full effort
is full victory."*

— Mohandas Gandhi

Steve Smith

Dikembe Mutombo

"Anything you want to accomplish you must have desire and love or you won't succeed. You have to want to work and repeat work and increase your effort on an everyday basis."

"I saw successful people when I came to this country and set myself a goal to be successful. You have to set goals and then try to reach them by hard work."

Tyrone Corbin

"A strong faith in God and yourself and a willingness to work hard and be patient will give you success."

Steve Smith

"Everyone's talent is about the same in the pros. What keeps you here is the time you put in studying and practicing longer. Keep doing the things you can do well and work on your weaknesses."

"My mother told me to KISS. 'Keep it simple, Steve. You get more out of life that way.'"

Mookie Blaylock

"You've got to work at it every day. Respect yourself. Get your rest and take care of your body."

Christian Laettner

"Catch the ball and look to pass first."

"Stay in school and get as much education as you can."

Dominant personality
Mookie Blaylock

Care-giver
Steve Smith

BOSTON CELTICS

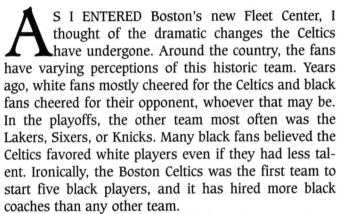

AS I ENTERED Boston's new Fleet Center, I thought of the dramatic changes the Celtics have undergone. Around the country, the fans have varying perceptions of this historic team. Years ago, white fans mostly cheered for the Celtics and black fans cheered for their opponent, whoever that may be. In the playoffs, the other team most often was the Lakers, Sixers, or Knicks. Many black fans believed the Celtics favored white players even if they had less talent. Ironically, the Boston Celtics was the first team to start five black players, and it has hired more black coaches than any other team.

Boston's Bill Russell became the first black NBA coach in 1966.* Charles "Chuck" Cooper joined the Celtics, along with Washington's Earl Lloyd and New York's Nat "Sweetwater" Clifton to integrate the league in the 1950-51 season.

Since the opening of the Fleet Center, the so-called Celtic pride and the arrogance of the Celtics' fans have diminished. Their green and white uniforms and the infamous parquet floor are the only remnants of an era gone by.** The old Celtics are tucked away in historic tradition except for the venerable Spider. This amicable man has swept the floor at halftime through the dynasties and into the present lean years.

The Celtics had a pride and mystique on the court that only a Celtic could fully understand. It took me five years in the NBA to decide if I believed in the pride. I concluded that their pride was based on their success and that their success was based on their willingness to sacrifice individual goals for the good of the team. The Celtic players thought as a unit and made good decisions quickly. In the vernacular of Spike Lee, they would

*John McLendon was actually the first black coach of professional basketball. In 1961 he coached the Cleveland Pipers of the short-lived American Basketball League.

**The parquet floor has bumps, cracks and low spots that interfere with ball control.

always "do the right thing."

Their front line of Larry Bird, Robert Parish, Kevin McHale and Cedric "Cornbread" Maxwell seemed choreographed without a confining script. I could never figure exactly why Dennis Johnson was so effective. I just knew you couldn't beat him. Former Buck's coach Don Nelson said once that Johnson "has the ability to stay with you without moving as fast as you are."

I understood exactly what he meant. Red Auerbach said the Bulls of the '90s closely resemble the old Celtics. I think he meant that the Bulls also have excellent choreography with a flexible script (the triple post offense) and they think as a unit.

"I never wanted them to forget Babe Ruth. I just wanted them to remember Henry Aaron."

— Henry Aaron

_____

Dana Barros
"Always remember what it took to get here. Let negative statements be fuel for your success."

"Realize how fortunate you are and don't take things for granted. Stay humble."

Pervis Ellison
"Coach George Raveling said, and I agree, 'No matter what you do give 100 percent, that's all that counts.'"

"I like how Donnie Simpson ends his show. 'Shoot for the moon because if you fall short you'll still be among the stars.'"

Dee Brown
"Hard work gets you to the next level. It'll never hurt anyone. It'll get you over the hump. Extra effort is a key. Otherwise you can drift or fade away."

"I've seen great players pass on and leave this team. Basketball is fun and is my job, but life and family are very important. Live to the fullest, you never know what'll happen the next day. Look what happened to Reggie (Lewis). Leave basketball on the court."

Rick Fox

"In team sports, learn to communicate, work together and accept your role. I learned from a great high school and college coach that the team is the most important thing."

"Choices that you make now will affect your future. Realize that, regardless of your age, and it will help you to make good choices."

Rick Fox

"Once you say you're going to settle for second, that's what happens to you in life, I find.

— John F. Kennedy

Dino Radja

"Having friends is the most important thing in life and being healthy."

"You have to work hard and that will pay off sooner or later. How hard you work determines how good you'll be."

Dominant personality
Rick Fox

Care-giver
Rick Fox

"Passion is not friendly. It is arrogant, superbly contemptuous of all that is not itself, and, as the very definition of passion implies the impulse of freedom, it has a mightly intimidating power. It contains a challenge. It contains an unspeakable hope."

— James Baldwin

CHARLOTTE HORNETS

C HARLOTTE HAS TWO players who are practically opposite in the way they relate to people. Tyrone "Mugsy" Bogues shares smiles, hugs, thoughts, and his happiness. He could be called a people person. Anthony Mason is non-demonstrative and self-contained. He could easily be called an introvert.

The 5'3" Bogues is disarming, easy to interview and charms his audiences. He is an entertainer with style. Bogues could join the Harlem Globetrotters after his NBA career and continue to be an ambassador for the game. He is also the life of the locker room.

"I learned never to listen to Mugsy," chuckled former teammate Larry Johnson, giving Bogues a big smile.

Mason doesn't go out of his way to give interviews. He intimidates his opponents with physical in-your-face basketball. He'd rather be respected for his work than his charm. He is a gladiator. His strength comes from within and from his personal relationship with Jesus. Both Mason and Bogues are a credit to the game.

Coach Dave Cowens, a rookie head coach, had to establish an identity for his new team. After the Alonzo Mourning trade, teams considered the Hornets soft with few good defensive players. Their assistant coach, T. R. Dunn, who once made a living playing defense, would probably have been their best defensive player even in retirement. They had sweet-shooting wing players in Dell Curry and Glen Rice. But to have a meal you need more than "hot wings."

Mason was somewhat of a savior as he gave them a defensive presence and leadership. Rice and Curry quickly found out what Earl "The

Pearl" Monroe discovered about Wes Unseld. When Unseld picked (set up a screen), you stayed picked. There was no getting around him quickly. Monroe had a lot of time to prepare his shot. Now Rice and Curry also have that luxury of time, even though neither needed more than an instant.

The fans seem to miss the emotional involvement of Mourning and Johnson, but they're starting to appreciate the new mix.

———————————

"No man is an island, entire of itself, every man is a piece of the continent, a part of the main. ... Any man's death diminishes me because I am involved in mankind, and therefore never send to know for whom the bell tolls; it tolls for thee."

— John Donne

Tyrone "Mugsy" Bogues
"Being around good people can help you to form your career."

"Education can enhance your life and help you to succeed."

Mugsy Bogues

"When one door of happiness closes, another opens, but often we look so long at the closed door that we do not see the one which has opened for us."

— *Helen Keller*

Vlade Divac
"Most important thing is to be around good coaches and players. You can learn a lot from them."

"Most importantly I had a goal and a dream. I didn't know if I could reach it or not but I had a goal. Now my dreams have come true but I still have goals."

Ricky Pierce
"Dedication. Working in the summer until it is over."

"Keep faith in God."

Glen Rice
"It is important to meet people throughout your life."

"Nothing is secure. You may be on the team one day and gone the next. Realize that pro basketball is a business."

Dell Curry
"My family comes first."

"Basketball is business, but you must have fun."

Anthony Mason
"Trust in the Lord and let it be known that he will take care of everything."

Dominant personality
Anthony Mason

Care-giver
Mugsy Bogues

"Nothing that God ever made is the same thing to more than one person. That is natural. There is no single face in nature, because every eye that looks upon, sees it from its own angle. So every man's spice-box seasons his own food."

— *Zora Neale Hurston*

Anthony Mason

CHICAGO BULLS

T HE REV. ANDREW Young, former Southern Christian Leadership Conference vice president under the Rev. Martin Luther King Jr., former ambassador to the United Nations, former Atlanta mayor, former congressman, former head of the Atlanta Chamber of Commerce, and former vice president of the Olympic organizing committee, often speaks on inclusion. He counsels heads of corporations and countries on the strength and beauty of diversity. Coach Phil Jackson and the Chicago Bulls could be his role models for success.

True diversity requires a sharing of power and a respect for the skills, intelligence and desires of others. Jackson has taken the domineering strength of Michael Jordan, the complete play of Scottie Pippen, and the intense emotionally charged play of Dennis Rodman to build a great team. Phil has done a great job of effectively applying input from his assistant coaches. Coach Tex Winter introduced the Bulls' triple post offense and former assistant coaches Johnny Bach and Jim Cleamons engineered the team's defensive schemes. Jackson's players have diverse backgrounds.

Pippen was one of 12 children. He attended college on a work-study program as a team equipment manager. He was allowed to practice with the team at Central Arkansas. Of course he went on to become that school's greatest player.

The fathers of two key NBA players were murdered. Jordan's father was killed in an apparent robbery, and Steve Kerr's father was assassinated in Beirut, Lebanon, where he was president of American University.

Kerr remembers the passion his dad had for the Middle East. "I remember clearly the Camp

David peace talks with (Egypt's President Anwar) Sadat, (Israeli Prime Minister Menachem) Begin and (U.S. President Jimmy) Carter. Dad was so excited about Middle East peace," says Kerr. "That's what he lived for."

As a kid, Kerr climbed the pyramids of Egypt and cruised the Nile.

Tony Kukoc grew up in Croatia, and Luc Longley is from Australia. Bill Wennington is a Canadian and Jud Buecheler is a professional beach volleyball player.

Rodman is easily the most eccentric Bulls player, but most everyone respects his work at the non-glamour jobs of defense, rebounding and physical play.

Jackson, whose spiritual background has included the study of Eastern and Western philosophy, has pulled together enough diversity to make Andrew Young proud.

Then there is Michael.

I like the way Hakeem Olajuwon describes him;

"Michael Jordan is like a big cat hopping upon a rock; as soon as he lands he goes straight up. People think he's going to a spot on the floor, but really the court is just a stepping stone. He gets the ball, hops to a space, and leaps. ... If he were an animal in the jungle, Michael could be out on the biggest rock and no one would disturb him, no one would attack him. He wouldn't have to watch his back. All the other animals would wait fearfully; they'd be scared even while he slept."

"The things and best people rise out of their separateness. I'm against a homogenized society because I want the cream to rise."

— Robert Frost

Scottie Pippen

"Play the game as a team. Your skills will naturally blossom as an individual."

"Take it one day at a time and enjoy it."

Dennis Rodman

"Keep your individuality."

"Keep a positive outlook on life regardless of how famous you are. Never lose your bearing."

Michael Jordan

"Let the game come to you, don't chase it. Set your own expectations."

"Enjoy every minute of life. Never second guess life."

"Success isn't something you chase. It's something you have to put forth the effort for constantly. Then maybe it'll come when you least expect it."

"If a man does not keep pace with his companions, perhaps it is because he hears a different drummer. Let him step to the music which he hears, however measured or far away."

— Henry David Thoreau

Michael Jordan

Tony Kukoc

"Work and practice hard. Try to enjoy the game. Don't see the game as work; it is just a game."

"Being with a team is like family. Be supportive especially when things aren't going well."

Luc Longley

"You have to stay positive and learn from positives and negatives and gain confidence."

"Perseverance pays."

Steve Kerr

"Basketball has taught me how to live my life better. Discipline and hard work are good teachers. Results are gratifying."

"Everyday I wake up excited to go to work. Find something in life that you enjoy. I know that may be hard but education can help you reach this goal."

Robert "Chief" Parish

"Keep everything in perspective and never be too high on yourself."

"Parental guidance is very important."

Dominant personality
Michael Jordan

Care-giver
Scottie Pippen

"It seems to me that one of the most vital questions that touches our American life is how to bring the strong, the wealthy, and the learned into helpful touch with the poorest, more ignorant, and humble and at the same time make the one appreciate the vitalizing, the strengthening influence of the other."

— Booker T. Washington

CLEVELAND CAVALIERS

T HE CAVS IS a team that no one wants to play. They defend the lane very well. Rarely can an opponent get to the basket or take an open shot. They walk the ball slowly up the floor and force their opponents to play at a slow tempo. The Cavs are a very disciplined team. Their actions are mostly calculated and rehearsed. Even though the beauty of basketball is creative spontaneity expressed skillfully and athletically, the Cavs have managed to manufacture excitement through intensity and choreography.

Terrell Brandon, a two-time all-star, is their best player and least typical Cavalier. He is small, creative, and a good open-court player. One would think that his talents would be inhibited with the Cavs' style of play. However, he has found a way to show his skills even in this controlled environment. He would be a star in any system.

Brandon, a preacher's son, seems confident but not cocky. He has compassion that probably came from both parents. However, he could still be called a mother's boy. His mom started the "Mothers of Professional Basketball Players Association." He still calls his parents after every game. Terrell is wise with his money.

He says, "People think I'm going to use my money to buy cars, but I'd rather give it to my church, to my family, do something I can be proud of. What can I do to make my son proud of me? What can I do so my parents will be proud of me?"

"You may fill your heads with knowledge, but unless it is based upon high upright character, upon a true heart, it will amount to nothing. You will be no better than the most ignorant."

— Booker T. Washington

Bobby Phills
"The main thing that I go by is never let anyone tell you what you cannot do. Believe in yourself. If you believe, you will achieve."

"Even off the court the same thing applies, have confidence in yourself."

Chris Mills
"The most important things are dedication and confidence. Know you can achieve it if you put your mind to it."

"Positiveness. In order to maintain it you have to have a background with the Lord."

Terrell Brandon
"Believe that you can be successful and don't give up. Strive to do the best you can. Believe you can accomplish whatever you want to accomplish."

"Believe in God first. Whatever you do give Him the credit."

Tyrone Hill
"A good work ethic. You can't make it without it. Success does not fall out of the sky. Stay hungry, never be satisfied."

"Don't take life for granted."

Mark West
"Always try to be better the next day than you were the day before. Work on strengths and weaknesses."

"In life the greatest power we have is the ability to choose. You can choose right from wrong, to persevere or to quit, that's your choice."

Terrell Brandon

"Men are what their mothers made them."

— Ralph Waldo Emerson

Dominant personality
Bobby Phills

Care-giver
Terrell Brandon

Bobby Phills

DALLAS MAVERICKS

T HE MAVERICKS HAVE been in transition for several years. They had some outstanding years in the infancy of the franchise. Appetites were aroused and expectations raised. But suddenly, injuries, unfortunate incidents and a few bad decisions brought them down. In trying to rebuild, they applied an old philosophy of success that says, "Realize what you're doing right and do more of it." Thus they tried to utilize three young talented players, Jamaal Mashburn, Jason Kidd and Jim Jackson, to their fullest. Success never came and they had to find a way to start over.

Their first-year head coach, Jim Cleamons, and I were teammates on the New York Knicks. I've never seen a player who was more a student of the game than Jim. Every time we ate lunch together it turned into a strategy session. He analyzed the team as well as our guard play. I learned many basketball lessons from Jim and I knew that he'd make an excellent coach one day. Even as an analyst, I'd talk to him and he would want to explain the marvel of the Bulls' triple post offense. But when he was no longer a Bulls assistant coach, he had to sell his discipline, passion and ideas to a new group of athletes.

Don Nelson, a three-time NBA Coach of the Year and now the Mavericks' general manager, once said, "You have to be totally dedicated to your job and have it as one of your very, very, high priorities. We're talking one-two-three here — family, religion and coaching. Coaching has got to be in your top three or otherwise you're not going to be successful." Cleamons has that kind of dedication to coaching. Together they can find a way. But if they are to succeed in the near future, they'll need a big contribution from their new center Shawn Bradley.

Bradley has had a rough road in the NBA. Everyone had extremely high expectations for him because of his high position in the draft. I wondered what he would say about success and how he viewed himself. He gave me great definitions for success and love. He is grounded and knows exactly what is important in life. I don't think he'll be overly affected by fans or media.

"The Celtics played together because we all knew that it was the best way to win. Each player was as competitive as Atilla the Hun, and if individual combat would have won championships, we'd have been fighting each other. I think we liked each other because we liked each other, and we won because we knew how to. "

— Bill Russell

A. C. Green
"There's always another game."

"Your identity can't be totally basketball."

Robert Pack
"Be confident and sure of yourself. That and hard work will help you."

"Be positive about everything, your children, your career and your life. Regardless of whatever tough situation you face, you can succeed by maintaining a positive attitude."

Shawn Bradley

Shawn Bradley

"I learned that success is determined when you look in the mirror and you've given 110 percent. The outcome doesn't determine success."

"I was taught God loved me and my mother loved me and even if my mom didn't, God did and nothing else matters."

Shawn Bradley

"A close look at any athletic competition and especially at facial expressions and body language reveals that many individuals or even entire teams go into momentary lapses of confidence that often prove disastrous. The ever-threatening danger is that a momentary lapse will begin to deepen almost on its own accord."

— Arthur Ashe

Derek Harper

Derek Harper
  "It is important to remain humble. Don't get caught up in yourself."

  "Prepare and it will take away your fear of being on stage. Depending on luck causes the fear."

Michael Finley
  "The key is always giving 110 percent while on the court. Whether it is offense or defense, that extra effort helps me to be successful."

  "I feel that you only get out of life what you put into it. It takes hard work to be successful."

Dominant personality
Derek Harper

Care-giver
A.C. Green

DENVER NUGGETS

LAPHONSO ELLIS AND Dale Ellis have both had to re-energize their careers. A pro basketball player is very fortunate when he is cast in a certain role and allowed to play that role his entire career. More often than not, adjustments are the beginning of the end of an NBA career. It is very difficult to be successful in a new environment with different personnel. But it is a rare occurrence to find players that can develop new strengths and compete on the NBA level.

Dale Ellis was a first team All-American his senior year at the University of Tennessee. He averaged 22 1/2 points and shot 60 percent from the field. He played practically the whole season in the low post with his back to the basket. He has since taken his game outside where he has become the NBA's all-time leader in three-point field goals made and attempted. He's won the Long Distance Shoot Out, made the all-star team, and won the NBA's Most Improved Player award. By watching the Nuggets in pregame warm-ups, it is obvious why he's been successful. He never takes a jumper for granted as he is always working on his shot. He actually works up a sweat while fine tuning his shot.

LaPhonso Ellis was unstoppable on the low post before knee injuries stalled his career. When he returned, a new power forward, Antonio McDyess, would have his name on the block. LaPhonso decided that his future may be as a small forward. He dramatically increased his range and mobility. Until Juwan Howard made similar changes to his game over a summer, I'd never seen such a phenomenal adjustment in style from one year to the next. LaPhonso is a very spiritual person.

LaPhonso Ellis
"Trust in Jesus."

"You reap what you sow. Hard work that you put in will give God a fruitful harvest. You cheat in preparations you fall short of the glory."

Antonio McDyess
"I believe in myself. I believed that I could do it. Keep your dreams alive."

"Ask God who made you to keep on remaking you."

— *The Rev. Norman Vincent Peale*

"Pray and believe in God. Leave life in His hands."

Kenny Smith
"Stability brings success. The more stable, the more successful you can become."

"To be good is not enough when you dream of being great."

Vincent Askew
"You have to do something well. Defense, scoring or whatever. You have to specialize in something."

"Whatever hard times you go through, you have to have faith in God and yourself. You will always have doubters."

LaPhonso Ellis

"The ideas I stand for are not mine. I borrowed them from Socrates. I swiped them from Chesterfield. I stole them from Jesus and I put them in a book. If you don't like their rules, whose would you use?"

— Dale Carnegie

Dominant personality
Laphonso Ellis

Care-giver
Laphonso Ellis

Dale Ellis

DETROIT PISTONS

USUALLY WHEN I hear comments that a player does the intangibles well, I assume that the player doesn't have much talent. This would be a false assumption concerning players on this team. There are three players who are exceptional in this regard, Joe Dumars, Otis Thorpe and Grant Long. Intangibles are things that don't show up in the box scores or game statistics. Examples are reversing the ball, blocking out and allowing a teammate to rebound and properly executing game plans. If a team has a good coach, a good game plan and a star to rally around, these players will win a lot of games for the team. Detroit has all of the above.

If you were to ask me to list the qualities of a perfect shooting guard, I'd say, he has to be a good shooter, he has to know how to come off screens, catch and shoot without a dribble. He has to execute a pick-and-roll well. He has to play good defense and make good decisions especially at clutch time. He should show good sportsmanship on the floor and be a good citizen off the floor. Doesn't this sound like Joe Dumars? I've always respected Dumars because he's always stayed within the character of Joe Dumars. It didn't matter if he were playing with "The Bad Boys," a team on the decline, or an up-and-coming team; he was a professional shooting guard.

Grant Hill is an example of the power of positive parental influence. He has obviously inherited talent and size. But through his parents' guidance, he has learned how to combine qualities that almost oppose each other. He has formed a unique style. In his game he is aggressive, yet patient. He has street basketball savvy and toughness but he also has textbook and clinical fundamentals. He's athletically creative, yet he is very controlled. I'll bet he could mix classical music with hip hop and come up with a new form that both cultures would like. He could be the Arthur Ashe of basketball. He has that kind of crossover appeal. His dad, Calvin, was an all-star running back in the NFL and a Yale graduate. His mom, Janet, is an attorney and a graduate of Radcliffe. Early in Hill's life, one of his friends called Janet the "General."

"Everyone liked her because she was nice but everyone feared her too," said Hill. "She could be tough." He calls her the Michael Jordan of mothers.

As Hill put it, "Michael Jordan can do everything and is best at everything he does. That's the way I look at my mother." In every interview I've had with Hill, his respect, gratitude and compassion shine through. He has been taught well.

"The things which are seen are temporal, but the things which are unseen are eternal. The hidden things stand for character and the temporal things are those which stand for reputation. The more important things are those which are hidden."

— Booker T. Washington

Otis Thorpe
"You are as good as your last game."

"Take it one day at a time."

Joe Dumars
"Treat everyone as you want to be treated every day."

"Whatever you put in you'll get out. If you put a lot of work in you'll get a lot of success; if not, you'll get a little."

Terry Mills
"Being prepared to play every day is mandatory to your success."

"You'll face obstacles every day, so take it one day at a time."

Grant Hill

"My parents taught me if you work hard, work together, and try to get along, you can succeed."

"Luck comes from working hard."

Grant Hill

"I shall study how I may be tender without being soft; gracious without being ingratiating; kind without being sentimental; and understanding without being judgmental."

— *The Rev. Howard Thurman*

Lindsey Hunter
"Regardless of what happens, keep your self confidence."

"My father says and I believe, nothing good comes easy. You have to work hard for what you want."

Grant Long
"Stay humble and stay hungry."

"My motto in life is dream, because dreams are visions of things to come."

Dominant personality
Grant Hill

Care-giver
Joe Dumars

Joe Dumars

GOLDEN STATE WARRIORS

T HROUGH ALL THE changes and transition for the Golden State Warriors, there has been one constant in Chris Mullin. He has had his ups and downs and injuries, but he has always been resilient enough to bounce back and land on his feet.

The essence of basketball is twofold. It is positioning and rhythm. Just as Karl Malone embodies the position concept, Mullin represents the rhythm. As do most New York City players, Mullin has a flow to his game. This flow is a God-given talent that is improved by playing against live competition. It cannot be taught by drills, textbooks or film. In earlier days, Gail Goodrich and Earl "The Pearl" Monroe were masters of the rhythm game. Their shots were rarely blocked, yet they didn't jump very high nor have blinding speed. They were like snake charmers that brought you into a hypnotic rhythm and deceitfully shot or faked and left you frozen. The "Pearl" would say, "Just look in their eyes and go on and shoot. They can't block it." I never fully understood how Goodrich led the 1971-72 championship Lakers in scoring. I finally played against him in my rookie year and found his shot impossible to time. It just happened without warning. Now Mullin has all the tricks of a gym rat and is an outstanding pure shooter.

Mullin is a workaholic who keeps in good shape and can run all game long. His hero as a youngster was John Havlicek. There are similarities in their games as well as their number (17). Mullin led the NBA in minutes played two straight seasons and scored more than 25 points per game in five straight seasons. Coach Rick Adelman says, "He just makes everyone better around him.

It seems like he sees things before they happen. He's better than I thought he was. I don't think you appreciate him until he's on the floor and you see him every day."

"If you have no prejudice, no bias, if you are open, then everything around you becomes extraordinarily interesting, tremendously alive. ... If you can observe alertly, keenly, but without judging, without concluding, you will find that your thinking becomes astonishingly acute. Then you are learning all the time."

— Krishnamurti

B. J. Armstrong
"Appreciate every day of your life."

"Expect the unexpected."

Joe Smith
"You must work hard every night in life or business."

"You have to learn to work well with a lot of different people."

Chris Mullin
"Preparation."

"Prepare to win in advance, especially in the off-season."

"Manage ups and downs. Don't get too happy when you win or lose. Enjoy the game."

Latrell Sprewell
"When things are rough, never quit; sometimes you can get over the hump."

"Learn to anticipate what your opponents may do on the court and in life."

Bimbo Coles
"A lot of hard work pays off. I have put my life into basketball. It is not a job. It is something that I love. You have to love to compete every day."

"My family is my success. My daughter and my wife are important. I want to provide for my daughter and teach her right from wrong and to work hard."

Chris Mullin

"When you see a worthy person, endeavor to emulate him. When you see an unworthy person, then examine your inner self."

— *Confucius*

Dominant personality
Chris Mullin

Care-giver
B.J. Armstrong

Latrell Sprewell

HOUSTON ROCKETS

HAKEEM "THE DREAM" Olajuwon is very proud of his Nigerian heritage. He is also shaped strongly by his Islamic religion and his tribe, the Yorubas. Of all his family's proud influences, Olajuwon seems to have been shaped mostly by his mother. He says, "Devout Muslims pray five times a day and sometimes I would wake up before sunrise to go to the bathroom and I would find my mother on the prayer mat. ... Weekends I'd see her getting ready as I was going out to the field to play, and I would play for a long time and then get hungry and come back inside and see her still sitting there."

When Olajuwon planned to come to America to visit potential colleges and maybe sign a scholarship offer, he asked his parents for permission and money. He says, "I sat with her as she counted out the cash from her bankroll. This was principal, savings, money you did not spend. The ticket cost around $4,500. She gave me all the money she had."

Olajuwon's respectful demeanor is admired by the media and everyone else. When speaking of Yoruba traditions, he said, "People are proud of their background and their homes. Everywhere you go you represent your family, and if you show a lack of home training you are insulting not only yourself but your mother and father and your entire line. So you have to behave in public and in private in a way that brings honor and not disgrace upon you and your family. That's a requirement."

His discipline and diverse influences have helped him elevate the center position to a new level. His creativity has prevented him from accepting the role of a traditional center. He sees himself as a complete basketball player rather than only a center. And because of Olajuwon, fall-away baseline jumpers and dream shakes are everyday occurrences at least for "The Dream."

Hakeem Olajuwon
"Desire is the key. That should be your base. It is the driving force that leads to work ethics."

"To be God conscious is the foundation of life. It is the rock upon which we build."

Clyde Drexler
"Before you can succeed you have to learn how to fail. You learn to bounce back and learn from every time you try."

"Go through life trying to treat people the way you'd like to be treated at all times."

Charles Barkley
"The amount of time and effort you put into our game will determine how successful you are."

"There are no shortcuts, no handouts. You can be as successful as you want to be."

Kevin Willis
"Work ethic is the key to success and believing in yourself."

"Believe in God and you can be successful."

Eddie Johnson
"Communicate well and often."

"Work hard."

"There is a quiet courage that comes from an inward spring of confidence in the meaning and significance of life. Such courage is an underground river; flowing far beneath the shifting events of one's experience, keeping alive a thousand little springs of action."

— The Rev. Howard Thurman

"If one's reputation is a possession, then of all my possessions, my reputation means most to me."

— *Arthur Ashe*

Hakeem Olajuwon

Dominant personality
Hakeem Olajuwon

Care-giver
Clyde Drexler

Charles Barkley

INDIANA PACERS

T HE PACERS HAVE a hard time getting a lot of respect. They've had very good teams for years but have never been a favorite team of the media. The Pacers have a proud tradition of great players, winning teams, and fans that appreciate the game. Part of their difficulty comes from the fact that their heritage includes the American Basketball Association (ABA). Even though they won championships and had out-standing players, many traditional hard-core NBA fans never gave the former ABA teams their prop-er respect.

Four former ABA teams, the New Jersey Nets, the San Antonio Spurs, the Denver Nuggets, and the Indiana Pacers joined the NBA the same year. Pacers' coach, Larry Brown, has successfully coached all of these teams and played in the ABA himself. The Pacers have done a good job keeping the memories of their stars alive. They've retired the numbers of Mel Daniels, Roger Brown and George McGinnis. These were all great players and I'm glad to see them remembered.

Reggie Miller has brought a lot of attention and success to the Pacers. He brings the trash talk of the playground and a touch of Hollywood. He lights a fire under the Pacers, especially dur-ing the playoffs. The fundamental blue-collar style of the Pacers serves as a perfect backdrop for Miller's artistry. Somehow even Miller was overlooked for the 1997 All-Star Game. I guess he'll have to keep scoring and keep talking to get attention for himself and the team.

"The little praises I have received does not affect me unless it be to make me work furiously. Instead of a pillow to rest upon, it is a goal to prod me. I know that I can only get into the sunlight by work and only remain there by more work."

— Zora Neale Hurston

Mark Jackson
"Be persistent. Repetition is a key."

"Practice and attempt to master your craft."

"Trust in God."

Derrick McKey
"Follow parents advice."

"Get involved in a lot of activities, not only sports."

Antonio Davis
"Success starts with effort. Give 110 percent on the floor whether it's practice, a game, or shoot-around. You can always improve."

"The key is having a great foundation, mentally, physically and spiritually."

Rick Smits
"I'm not successful yet. Once we get to the championship, then I'll consider myself successful."

"Strive to be happy. For some people it's money, some, it's spiritual, some, it's family. Find what makes you happy."

Jalen Rose
"Never disrespect the game of basketball. It has opened a lot of avenues for me . . . travel , dreams, etc."

"Know what you want in life and strive to achieve it. There are more doubters than supporters. Give yourself a chance to be successful and don't settle for mediocrity."

Reggie Miller

"To be successful it is important to learn how to communicate with people."

"Manage your time well, practice hard, and make sacrifices."

Reggie Miller

"Nothing splendid has ever been achieved except by those who dared believe that something inside them was superior."

— Unknown

Duane Ferrell

"I always had a dream and it stayed with me even though I wasn't drafted. People said I had an in-between size and could not shoot well enough, but I always believed I could make it."

"Growing up, I always found people that I respected and modeled myself after them."

Dominant personality
Reggie Miller

Care-giver
Mark Jackson

LOS ANGELES CLIPPERS

C OACH PAT RILEY is credited with saying, "There's winning and there's misery." This suggests that those are the only two choices when playing or coaching basketball. Bill Fitch and Jerome "Pooh" Richardson would probably disagree. Fitch would add building, competing or turning a franchise around. He is the only NBA coach who has lost more than 1,000 games. (He has also won more than 900. Only three coaches have won more.) He has also survived triple-bypass heart surgery. Why would he continue to coach the Clippers if winning and misery were his only choices? We should note that the Clippers had some good teams and winning records in their history, but not lately. Fitch took the expansion Cleveland Cavaliers to three playoff appearances. He took a Boston Celtics team that had won only 29 games and had a 32-game turnaround. The following year, the Celtics won an NBA championship. Fitch took a Houston Rockets team that won 14 games and, in his third year, led them to the NBA finals with a 51-53 record.

Richardson has an ability to stay up and expect the best from some difficult situations. In his first three years in the NBA, he played in all 82 games each year with the Minnesota Timberwolves. The Wolves were an expansion team with a very demanding coach, Bill Musselman. In spite of frequent losses, Richardson always played hard and had a pleasant demeanor. If you didn't know better, you'd have thought he was playing for the Chicago Bulls. Richardson never hid and always carried himself and his team with pride. Despite the derogatory jokes about the Clippers in recent years, people like Pooh and Fitch improve their

Pooh Richardson

image. After all, Jerome's grandmother gave him the name "Pooh" after the storybook character. How could anyone called "Pooh" be anything but a pleasure to be around?

Pooh Richardson

"We are all lucky to be here. Obstacles for one man is a burden for someone else. Regardless of how hard the road seems, there is always a tougher road for someone else."

"Uncle Will Young taught me that you care for others with love and respect as you want others to care for you."

Rodney Rogers

"Being coachable is important. Coaches have been there and know what they are talking about, take time and listen to them. It will help."

"You have to grow up quick. You can't sit around and take it easy. You have to attack life head on. It's a tough job."

Malik Sealy

"Basketball is like life. All the hard work that you put in gives off good results."

"My mom always told me it is a mighty poor rat that only has one hole. Expand your options."

Brent Barry

"To change your game you must change your work habit. I got that from Chris Mullin. He works hard."

"Yesterday is a canceled check, tomorrow is a promissory note, today is the only cash you have, spend it wisely."

Loy Vaught

"The harder I work, the luckier I get. I wasn't blessed with natural ability. I take a lot of extra shots, and don't give up on a rebound. The rebounding award that I received for this team was because of my hard work."

Loy Vaught

"Character is that which can do without success."

— Ralph Waldo Emerson

LaMond Murray

"Never stop working."

"Always stay mentally strong."

Dominant personality
Loy Vaught

Care-giver
Pooh Richardson

"I asked God for strength that I might achieve. I was made weak that I might learn humbly to obey. I asked for health that I might do greater things. I was given infirmity that I might do better things. I asked for riches that I might be happy. I was given poverty that I might be wise. I asked for all things that I might enjoy life. I was given life that I might enjoy all things. I got nothing I asked for . . . but everything I had hoped for almost despite myself, my unspoken prayers were answered. I am, among men, most richly blessed."

— Roy Campanella

LOS ANGELES LAKERS

MAGIC JOHNSON AND Jerry West have
helped to raise the level of excellence for
the Lakers. They have sustained their
effort for many years without being involved with
any other team. They have been loyal to the
Lakers and vice-versa. Long-term, two-way loyal-
ty is a rare and respected commodity. Of course
there have been other Laker greats with huge
impacts. The stars of their organization would
probably beat the stars of any other. Consider a
team with Johnson, West, Wilt Chamberlain,
Kareem Abdul-Jabbar and Elgin Baylor. I don't
believe any other organization could match that
lineup. But Johnson and West are still actively
contributing. For 15 years, West has been at the
top of the Lakers' basketball operations. He has
been affiliated with their six championships. In
his own right, he was a great player with a career
scoring average of 27 points per game and 10
selections to the all NBA first team. His greatest
impact now is in the decision-making area. He
found a way to sign Shaquille O'Neal and
acquired Kobe Bryant in a trade. To sign O'Neal
was an easy decision that required a lot of
maneuvering and money. But Bryant was a different story.

Bryant was 17 and fresh out of high school.
West had long held to the philosophy that high
school players should go to college before joining
the NBA. Perhaps it was the parent in him that
fostered this thinking. However, he made an
exception when he traded for Bryant. As vice
president of the Lakers' basketball operations,
West felt compelled to pursue Bryant if he became
available. After all, Bryant was not your typical
17 year-old. If there is such a thing as mature at

17, then that describes Bryant. His dad, Joe Bryant, had played in the NBA and abroad. Kobe had been around pro basketball all his life. He speaks fluent Italian and has outstanding basketball skills.

West knew that somehow this intelligent youngster should be a Laker. Bryant's mom and dad gave him input but allowed him to make the decision about going pro. After talking to him and watching him play, I agree with West. I hope that my son, Michael, now 3 years old, will be able to make responsible and intelligent decisions when he is 17. I hope he'll have the courage to follow his dreams. Joe Bryant, you did a good job.

West called Magic Johnson the greatest general that the NBA has known. His leadership abilities made everyone around him better. He could always find a way to win. The Lakers averaged 59 victories per season during the Johnson era. He was league MVP three times and orchestrated the showtime offense. The Lakers averaged 114 points per game during Johnson's first 12 years with the team. The 6-foot -9 point guard revolutionized that position and modified the way the game was played on the West Coast. Before there was Jordan, everyone wanted to be like Johnson. The young guards copied Johnson's techniques, throwing no-look passes and running the fast break. His influence is still felt on the Lakers and throughout the conference. Johnson also helped to make pro basketball popular. There was a time in the late '70s when attendance was low, television ratings were horrible and the game was suffering. We needed a hero. Then there was Magic! He was talented and exciting to watch, but more importantly he brought charisma and compassion to the game. Magic shared! He shared the ball with his teammates. Everyone said he was so unselfish. He shared his emotions and feelings during the game and interviews. He answered questions with enthusiasm, stories, and smiles.

"We are what we repeatedly do. Excellence then is not an act but a habit."

- Aristotle

He displayed a spirit of inclusion that spread to the fans. They were a part of the game. He often talked about keeping the crowd involved. Passing is an act of compassion and Johnson passed well.

Johnson may have been the ultimate caregiver as well as one of the most dominant players in the history of basketball. He continues to share

Shaquille O'Neal

"Sometimes much energy is spent in a vain attempt to protect one's self. We withdraw from participation in the struggles of our fellows because we must not get caught in the communal agony of those around us. We take no stand where fateful issues are at stake because we dare not run the risk of exposure to attack. But all this at long last is of no avail. The attack from without is missed and we escape only to find that the life we have protected has slowly and quietly sickened deep within because it was cut off from the nourishment of the Great Exposure."

— *The Rev. Howard Thurman*

his leadership and compassion by opening theaters in neighborhoods that other businesses are abandoning or neglecting.

History has taught us that there are no impartial observes. We are either part of the problem or part of the solution. Johnson finds ways to be part of the solution, and he teaches us lessons in caring.

Together Johnson and West helped the Laker organization to earn the Associated Press Professional Sports Franchise of the Decade honor. I'm not surprised.

"You cannot accept somebody else's premise on what your life could be."

— Nikki Giovanni

Magic Johnson
"You have to give 125 percent. Put your heart and soul into it. Learn to have a winning attitude. Don't accept losing but learn from your losses."

"Dream! Be a big dreamer and try to attain your dreams. Have fun! Every day is a gift from God. enjoy it!"

Nick Van Excel
"A lot of things distract you. Keep a level head. Be a leader, not a follower. And sometimes your friends aren't good leaders. Know how important they are in your success. Their support means a lot."

Shaquille O'Neal
"Be a leader not a follower. No matter what the circumstance, follow your dream."

"My father told me, dream with the ball, sleep with the ball, take care of the ball and keep practicing."

Robert Horry
"Believe in yourself. when I was coming up, no one thought I could do it. I was clumsy. Just keep practicing and don't get down on yourself. It's one step at a time."

"Just be honest with yourself and the people around you. Nobody likes a liar and a cheat."

Elden Campbell
"Stay true to your game. Know what your bread and butter is. Use that to the fullest."

"Take care of business. Everyone knows what they need to do. It's a matter of doing it."

Eddie Jones
"Mainly have a right attitude and good character. One thing they can't take away is courage and character. The things that you carry with you are the most important."

"Family is important."

Byron Scott
"Care about your teammates more than you care about yourself. You have to give something up to get something back."

"Treat everyone equally. Treat them the way you want to be treated."

George McCloud
"Discipline is the key."

"Value life itself more than awards or money or fame."

Kobe Bryant
"Follow your dreams. If you want to accomplish something, follow your dreams and go 110 percent. Don't let anyone tell you that you can't."

Dominant personality
Shaquille O'Neal

Care-giver
Byron Scott

Eddie Jones

MIAMI HEAT

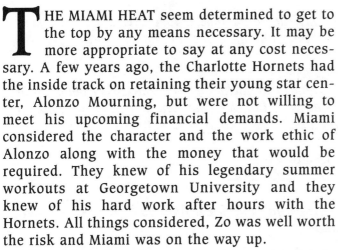

THE MIAMI HEAT seem determined to get to the top by any means necessary. It may be more appropriate to say at any cost necessary. A few years ago, the Charlotte Hornets had the inside track on retaining their young star center, Alonzo Mourning, but were not willing to meet his upcoming financial demands. Miami considered the character and the work ethic of Alonzo along with the money that would be required. They knew of his legendary summer workouts at Georgetown University and they knew of his hard work after hours with the Hornets. All things considered, Zo was well worth the risk and Miami was on the way up.

The Heat found a unique opportunity to acquire Tim Hardaway. Don Nelson had been quoted several years earlier saying Hardaway was his toughest player mentally and physically. Hardaway had overcome surgery on a torn anterior cruciate ligament in his knee and a torn scapholunate ligament in his left wrist. He still had the most compact unstoppable crossover dribble in the game. The Miami front office proved to be a good judge of character as well as talent.

P.J. Brown is their most underrated player. He had also been underrated with the New Jersey Nets. However, he won the Defensive Player of the Year award for the Nets. It should also be evident that it is hard to find a 6'11" forward who can defend small forwards as well as power forwards.

So once again, Miami's fortunes are based on good decisions as well as hard work. I wonder if Pat Riley were taught the fundamentals of investing in stocks, would he pick winners on Wall Street?

Alonzo Mourning

"Hard work and determination have always been the key to my success. I know someone is working just as hard as I am and that motivates me to work harder."

"Live life to the fullest. Take advantage of the positive things that life gives you. Life is short."

Keith Askins

"Find your niche and concentrate on doing what you do well. Practice time can be used on working on liabilities. Know your strengths."

"I am easily satisfied with the very best."

— Winston Churchill

Tim Hardaway
"Mental toughness."

"Have fun and learn from your friends and competitors."

Dan Majerle

"Perseverance. I overcame a lot of injuries. At times I wanted to give up, but I was able to turn things around. Don't give up."

"Have fun and try to make a positive difference in other people's lives."

Jamaal Mashburn

"Never take your situation for granted."

"Friendships are important."

Alonzo Mourning

*"We will either find
a way or make one."*

— Hannibal

Dominant personality
Alonzo Mourning

Care-giver
Tim Hardaway

Tim Hardaway

MILWAUKEE BUCKS

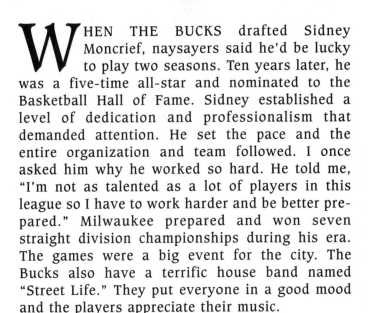

HEN THE BUCKS drafted Sidney Moncrief, naysayers said he'd be lucky to play two seasons. Ten years later, he was a five-time all-star and nominated to the Basketball Hall of Fame. Sidney established a level of dedication and professionalism that demanded attention. He set the pace and the entire organization and team followed. I once asked him why he worked so hard. He told me, "I'm not as talented as a lot of players in this league so I have to work harder and be better prepared." Milwaukee prepared and won seven straight division championships during his era. The games were a big event for the city. The Bucks also have a terrific house band named "Street Life." They put everyone in a good mood and the players appreciate their music.

Today the success of the Moncrief legacy is mostly dependent upon Vin Baker. Moncrief would absolutely approve of Baker and gladly hand him the baton. Baker has "game," as the players say. He also has character, tenacity, and confidence. His father is a Baptist minister and Baker grew up singing in his father's church choir. He missed four games early in the 1996-97 season because of an injury. It was the first time Baker had ever missed a game on any level of competition. He has also led the NBA in minutes played. But Baker is still learning and working on his game. He says, "I feel like I still haven't reached my potential. I feel like I have a lot more to learn and a lot better to get." Baker is not alone in the spiritual character department. Andrew Lang lives his faith and carries it around as part of his demeanor. He's also worked hard to make himself a solid player. During his senior year at the University of Arkansas, Lang averaged only 9.3 points per game. He's had to prove himself each year in the NBA.

Johnny Newman and Armon Gilliam are classic examples of solid veterans who get along, play hard and execute the coaches' game plan. They also get solid leadership from "General" Sherman Douglas. Sherman understands the game and gets as much from his natural talents as any player in the NBA.

Glenn Robinson is a very good player who is almost impossible to stop when he gets on a roll. He has the ability to come to a quick two-foot jump stop and immediately spring up and shoot the jumper. Unfortunately, unrealistic expectations were placed on him because of his contract and position in the draft. He could end up in a position similar to that of Dominique Wilkins, a scorer who may never be fully appreciated for his talent and work.

"Many persons have a wrong idea of what constitutes true happiness. It is not attained through self gratification, but through fidelity to a worthy purpose."

— Helen Keller

Andrew Lang

"When I first came to the NBA, I was told that a player should work on the things that he doesn't do well and the things he does well should be made a calling card."

"Seek ye first the Kingdom of God and all things will be yours. That doesn't necessarily mean that you'll have riches and fame, but you'll have peace of mind and happiness."

Armon Gilliam

"Regardless of the situation, good or bad, always strive to play well every night."

"Life has ups and downs, joys and sorrows, but focus on your faith and you'll be able to handle success and failure."

Vin Baker

"Never underestimate your abilities. You over-achieve because you feel you can."

"First and foremost, believe in God."

Vin Baker

"Happiness lies in the joy of achievement and the thrill of creative effort."

— *Franklin Roosevelt*

Sherman Douglas
"Give it your all at both ends of the court and good things will happen."

"Do unto others as you would have them do unto you, and respect other people."

Johnny Newman
"Always believe in yourself. Hard work will take you to levels you never thought you could reach."

"Being a good person and doing the right thing by people is one of the best things you can do."

Glenn Robinson
"Work hard and believe in yourself. You can only see how good you can be if you try your best. You can always improve."

"Everyone knows right from wrong. Do the right thing and never forget where you come from and the people behind you."

Ray Allen
"Working hard is more important than talent. You can overachieve."

"Have a plan, stick to it and stay focused."

Dominant personality
Vin Baker

Care-giver
Andrew Lang

MINNESOTA TIMBERWOLVES

KEVIN GARNETT, KOBE Bryant and Jermaine O'Neal are three young players who skipped college to go directly to the NBA. With all of the discussion of the league being too young, this group would be closely monitored. Kevin Garnett should receive an A+. His coaches rave that he is a team leader, an intelligent young man and an outstanding player. He made the All-Star Game in only his second year in the NBA. Most critics have recanted their statements. Now, not only is the NBA good for Kevin, he is good for the NBA.

Two important factors in anyone's success are having talent and being teachable. Kevin listens well. He had these comments concerning veteran and retired players

"The older guys want the younger guys to understand that they want to keep the game at the high pedestal they put it on. What they're doing is like if your son is not going to carry your family business like you want him to. That's their main concern, so they're going to think that. That should be a goal for us young guys to prove these older guys wrong. You have to look at them as they really care how this league is going, and we should care too."

Kevin is also a fan favorite in Minnesota as he patiently signs autographs, always has a smile, and is re-creating the small forward position. A 7-foot small forward is an oddity. However, he runs the floor, has ball-handling skills, and understands the game well enough to play the most athletic position in basketball.

Tom Gugliotta
"I've gotten out of basketball exactly what I've put in."

"How you deal with people is important. Treat them how you want to be treated."

Kevin Garnett
"Play hard."

"Have a positive attitude."

"Light tomorrow with today."

— Elizabeth Barrett Browning

Stephon Marbury
"Always work hard and stay mentally tough."

"Do unto others as you want them to do unto you."

Chris Carr
"Control the things that you can in terms of working out, staying prepared and being ready to play. The things that you can't control don't worry about."

"Keep your faith in God. things that you need to take care of, do so."

Doug West
"Hard work leads to all success."

Terry Porter
"The most important thing is being committed to win. Everyone must be committed, then it is easy."

"Mom and Dad always said, treat people the way you want to be treated."

Kevin Garnett

"I opened the doors of my school with an enrollment of five little girls whose parents paid me fifty cents weekly tuition . . . Though I hadn't a penny left, I considered cash money as the smallest part of my resources. I had faith in a living God, faith in myself and a desire to serve."

— Mary McLeod Bethune

Dominant personality
Tom Gugliotta

Care-giver
Kevin Garnett

"The universe is change. Our life is what our thoughts make it."

— *Marcus Aurelius*

Tom Gugliotta

NEW JERSEY NETS

S AM CASSELL HAS had a very difficult year to say the least. Just when it seemed that he was very secure at Houston, everything changed. He had to re-create himself several times over. The comfort in playing a particular role is knowing what is expected of you. You can then include personal and team goals and work toward making it all come together. Success early in your career can be deceptive. Anytime you become comfortable and think success is natural, you are setting yourself up for a potential fall.

Cassell has all the ingredients to succeed in spite of the difficulties. First of all he remains aggressive. He says, "I prepared myself the whole summer. I told myself I was going to be a starter. The kind of sparkplug role I played for three years in Houston was cool for the start of my pro career, but it's time for me to lift my horizons and evaluate where I want to be as a basketball player. I want to be a starter in this league." The second attribute is his toughness. He reminds me of John Starks. They both have a tough-minded approach to competing. Coach Danny Ainge said, "Sam's got a lot of energy and plays with a lot of confidence, plays with no fear."

Cassell actually was not surprised at his success in the NBA. He expected success and still does. The third attribute is hard work coupled with resiliency. Cassell picks an aspect of his game to work on each year.

"My first year I worked on my defense. My second year I was trying to get my offensive penetration (driving) down. My third year I was trying to finish moves to the basket. This year I'm working on understanding the keys to the whole role. I'm trying to think the game through," said Cassell.

Sam will do fine.

Kendall Gill has played for Charlotte on two occasions. He played for the Seattle Supersonics before coming to New Jersey.

Each time a player changes teams, he has to adjust to new environments on and off the court. The change of coaches also adds to the difficulty. Continuity and rhythm would help anyone to get to a comfort zone. Gill has been asked to play the point guard, the shooting guard, and the small forward positions. He has learned to focus his efforts regardless of the circumstances. He goes out and overachieves almost every night at the small forward position. He established The Kendall Gill House for the working homeless in Charlotte, N.C.

———————————————

"Most people resist change, even when it promises to be for the better. But change will come, and if you acknowledge this simple but indisputable fact of life, and understand that you must adjust to all change, then you will have a head start.

— Arthur Ashe

Sam Cassell

"Determination. Coming out of college no one but me thought I would be a good pro. I was very determined. If you have determination, the goal is not that hard to reach."

"You'll have obstacles. It is not predictable. you must take the good with the bad and keep striving. Life is not easy."

Chris Gatling

"Do your work early. Then you can relax."

"Have goals in life. I had one to make the all-star team. I realized a dream."

Kendall Gill
   "Stay humble."

   "Believe in yourself; it'll keep you progressing."

Kendall Gill

"Potential powers of creativity are within us and we have the duty to work assiduously to discover these powers."

— *The Rev. Martin Luther King Jr*

"A hundred times every day I remind myself that my inner and outer life depend on the labours of other men, living and dead, and that I must exert myself in order to give in the same measure as I have received."

— Albert Einstein

Kevin Edwards
"Never give up. I was cut from the team my freshman and sophomore years of high school. I did not try out my junior year. I finally made the team my senior year."

"Remember where you came from no matter the level of success."

Jim Jackson
"The biggest benefit from playing basketball is taking care of my family."

"It's important to relate to people on and off the court."

Reggie Williams
"Don't take things too seriously. You can lose big one night and win big the next night. There are a lot of games."

"Live one day at a time and respect others to get respect."

Jayson Williams
"Realize that your job is important. It is not a hobby. Stay conditioned mentally and physically."

Dominant personality
Kendall Gill

Care-giver
Jayson Williams

NEW YORK KNICKS

JOHN STARKS WOULD be on the NBA all-courage team. He attacks the game with everything that he has. He, along with Charles Oakley, has no reluctance to challenge bigger, or more talented, players. John also has the courage to face up and acknowledge past difficulties and discuss them with the media.

New Yorkers can appreciate the hard work and intense play of Starks. There is no "fixing to do something" in New York. It is do it right now with your best effort or lose your chance. Knicks fans even thought Pat Riley was a glamour and glitter prima donna. Later they learned to appreciate his hard work and dedication. They also seem to accept their less accomplished coach, Jeff Van Gundy, because of his work ethic.

Van Gundy, like many others, has a love-hate relationship with Starks. He said, "With John and I, it's always been love-hate. That can take place within the same minute or the same possession. I love the way he competes without fear, the way he plays with heart and desire."

When you realize that in two years Starks went from bagging groceries to playing for the New York Knicks, you better understand that his only chance for success was to out-work the long line of people in front of him.

Part of the attraction of playing for the New York Knicks is calling Madison Square Garden home. There is no better place to play basketball than the world's most famous arena when it is filled with energetic, intense, New York fans. There is pride in defending the honor of this magnificent arena that is taken seriously by Knicks' leaders. During the last year of his career, Earl Monroe played fewer minutes than usual. He had toned down his intensity and become an affable leader that everyone admired. Then all of a sudden after a home loss, he snapped. "The Knicks should have more have more pride than to go out and get embarrassed like this in this arena and take it lightly."

Coach Red Holtzman nodded in agreement and we all quietly listened and learned. Patrick Ewing now embodies the role of protector of the pride of Madison Square Garden.

———

"He who starts behind in the great race of life must forever remain behind or run faster than the man in front"

— Dr. Benjamin E. Mays

Charles Oakley
"As long as you can wake up every day, you can succeed."

"Be yourself and try to understand people. Don't put anyone down. Remember the people that are not as blessed as you are."

Allan Houston
"My dad taught me to have confidence in myself because no one could take that from me. Growing up I lived near Muhammad Ali and no one had more confidence than he."

"My mom taught me that everything happens for a reason. If you pray and have faith everything will work out."

Larry Johnson
"Never forget where you came from."

"Respect other people the way you want to be respected."

Buck Williams
"Regardless of talent or age you can't be afraid of hard work."

"I look at life as a roller coaster. Brace yourself and endure it. It'll make you a better person or break you. Adversity breeds character, and character breeds hope."

John Starks

"Work hard and envision yourself later on down the road being successful."

"You have to have faith and believe in God. You can always turn to Him."

John Starks

"I had to make my own living and my own opportunity. . . Don't sit down and wait for the opportunities to come; you have to get up and make them.

— Madame C.J. Walker

Patrick Ewing
"Hard work always pays off."

"Always believe in yourself even when others don't."

Dominant personality
Patrick Ewing

Care-giver
Larry Johnson

"The road to happiness lies in two simple principles, find what it is that interests you and that you can do well and when you find it put your whole soul into it — every bit of energy and ambition and natural ability you have."

— John D. Rockefeller III

Patrick Ewing

ORLANDO MAGIC

HOW DID THE Orlando Magic ever know that Penny Hardaway would be so good? With Chris Webber and Jamaal Mashburn also eligible, the Magic made a deal for Anfernee Hardaway. Sure he had outstanding credentials, but so did the others. Hardaway had been the Parade Magazine National High School Player of the Year and named "Mr. Basketball" in Tennessee. He averaged 36.6 points and 10 rebounds per game.

He had two outstanding years at Memphis State University, but he continued to get much better in the NBA. Hardaway, two-time all NBA first team selection, was the only player to accomplish all of the following: average 20-plus points (21.7), average five-plus assists (7.1) and shoot better than 50 percent from the floor (51 percent). His grandmother, who seemed to have all the love in the world for him, called him "Pretty." It sounded like "Penny" and the nickname stuck.

Nick Anderson, the first collegiate draft selection of the Magic, is the team's all-time leading scorer. I like the fact that he remembers his childhood friend and prep teammate Ben Wilson. Wilson was rated one of the nation's best high school players. He was tragically shot and killed. Anderson wears Wilson's number (25) in honor of his friend.

Horace Grant was an excellent addition to the Orlando Magic club. His work ethic is contagious and he impacts the game by out-working his opponent. Horace weighed only 207 pounds when he joined the NBA. He worked himself into a 245-pound power-house. He has always been a favorite of his teammates because he is innocent, brutally honest and cheerful. "General" Grant studies Greek mythology and likens himself to Hercules and Apollo. He is also influenced by his strong Christian beliefs.

Gerald Wilkins is an energizer. Because of the fame of his older brother, Dominique, he had never received much attention. He, however, makes a significant impact on his team. He has played 80-plus games in eight of 10 seasons. He's scored more than 10,000 points.

"What is success? I think it is a mixture of having a flair for the thing that you are doing, knowing that it is not enough, that you have got to have hard work and a certain sense of purpose."

— Margaret Thatcher

Dennis Scott
"Always play as hard as possible, luck will follow."

"No matter how much success, appreciate it, it may not last long."

Horace Grant
"Stay focused on your faith, put everything in perspective."

"Winning is important."

Nick Anderson
"Hard work pays off."

"Always believe in yourself."

Ron Seikaly
"Adversity makes you a better player and person if you keep fighting it.

"Sometimes you have to take a step back to realize that this is only a game. You must have fun, real life is waiting."

Penny Hardaway
"Never give up in anything — compete."

"Pray and stay humble."

Penny Hardaway

"A person can not succeed in anything without a good, sound body - a body that is able to stand up against hardships, that is able to endure. Have a time to go to bed and have enough self control to say to those who would persuade you to dissipate." "My time for rest has come and you must excuse me."

— Booker T. Washington

Gerald Wilkins

"Number one is be well-conditioned. Success requires energy, heart and drive. Without conditioning you can't play this game, college high school nor pro. Most well-conditioned athletes excel."

"Believe in yourself. Have a strong work ethic. Nothing comes easy."

"Nothing is given, everything is taken."

Dominant personality
Penny Hardaway

Care-giver
Horace Grant

Horace Grant

PHILADELPHIA 76'ers

ALLEN IVERSON CAN make an immediate impact on a basketball game or team. His quickness and athleticism make him almost impossible to defend. His background and experiences give him a unique insight into two diverse cultures. He has lived and been influenced by the hustle of street life, but he's also been embraced by the disciplined, prideful guidance of Georgetown University Coach John Thompson. Even former Virginia Governor Douglas Wilder, the nation's first and only black governor, has been a factor in Allen's success.

The Rev. Andrew Young told me that during the Civil Rights marches of the 60's, he and the Rev. Martin Luther King, Jr. would go to the playgrounds to play basketball. After this fellowship, they could more readily get cooperation and support for their nonviolent marches. Of course, King continued to live around people of average means and to dine in average places. But his tremendous impact was felt all over the world. Young, while mayor of Atlanta, would hear from his friends that had been jailed with him. They would remind him never to forget the lessons and experiences that they had learned and shared. Coaches Johnny Davis and Maurice Cheeks are both soft-spoken former point guards that have a wealth of knowledge to share. I hope they speak loudly and emphatically enough to get Allen's attention.

Iverson's toughness and self-reliance were absolutely necessary for him to arrive at his present success level. His friends and background are a source of comfort and trust. He is in a unique position to reach and help kids with a similar background whom even Thompson or Wilder can't influence. Iverson should keep his friends, but make sure that he learns all of the lessons that are available. And with these lessons, he should lead his friends.

"All life is interrelated. The agony of the poor impoverishes the rich, the betterment of the poor enriches the rich. We are inevitably our brother's keeper because we are our brother's brother.

- Rev. Dr. Martin Luther King Jr

Clarence Weatherspoon
"Basketball is humbling. There are great athletes here. You have to respect the game and your opponents to be prepared."

"In life do the things that will make you successful. Start in life for fun and then step up to new challenges."

Jerry Stackhouse
"Have a lot of confidence no matter what other people say."

"Stay focused on what you want in life. Set high goals and if you don't achieve those goals you'll still be in good shape."

Rex Walters
"Potential is a crazy word, but every day my goal is to reach my potential. I don't know exactly what my potential is but I try to chase that level every day."

"My father said, 'Try to do what is right. Every person knows the difference between right and wrong. Always try to do right and you'll avoid a lot of distractions.'"

Michael Cage
"Persistence in each athlete is important. Success is often a roller-coaster ride."

"Life off the court is consistent with what I do on the court. Also accept that all things are not perfect. Be able to overcome some things and accept others. Make the world a pleasant place to live."

Allen Iverson
"Play every game like it's your last."

"Try to make the best decisions that you can make. I try to make the decisions that will benefit me and my family the most. Decision-making is crucial."

Allen Iverson

"I alone am responsible for being a good human being. My religion is not and neither is my family nor my race nor the institutions around me."

- Bill Russell

Derrick Coleman
"The key is how much heart do you have. It is the most important. Talent without heart is nothing. The heart is what separates the true players form the others."

"Setting goals for yourself is important. I realize that everyone can't play basketball, but setting goals and trying to achieve them is important for anyone."

Dominant personality
Allen Iverson

Care-giver
Michael Cage

PHOENIX SUNS

JOHN "HOT ROD" Williams is one of the NBA's most coachable players. He is a faithful person with a respectful demeanor. Tree Rollins describes Williams as "one of the nicest guys you ever want to meet."

He remained available to Cleveland even when he was offered a lot more money to go elsewhere a few years ago. Williams stayed to learn the game from then Coach Lenny Wilkens. That was not a bad idea.

One of the best compliments that you can give a person is to say he can work with anybody. Kevin Johnson can play effectively with any other star and for any coach in the NBA. He can create a shot for himself or a teammate almost at will. For several years, Phoenix has maintained a potent offense. The quickness of Johnson has been the catalyst for the high octane offenses.

Johnson has also maintained a clear image of himself. He knows exactly who he is, what he has left and what he can accomplish. In talking to him, one doesn't sense any arrogance or an excessive ego. I asked him why he would retire with so many skills undiminished. He said, "This is how I want to go out." He knows what he is doing, but we'll miss him.

Jerry Colangelo has been instrumental in the success of the NBA and the Phoenix Suns. For the Suns, he's taken risks, made good decisions and led the organization with discipline and compassion. One of his best decisions was to involve and keep Cotton Fitzsimmons.

Fitzsimmons coached the Suns on three separate occasions. He always brought energy, passion and simplicity to the game. Players liked his style and respected his efforts. Fitzsimmons had confidence in the art and creativity of the game. He'd motivate players by challenging them and then trusting them to make positive things happen. He'd say things like "Come on! You're better than that." On the sidelines he was always in the game. He brought an energy that could pick the players up. It might

"A man whose thoughts are elsewhere will not fail to the inch to take always the same number and length of steps in the place where he walks; but if he goes at it attentively, measuring and counting them, he will find what he did naturally and by chance, he will not do as exactly by design.

— Michel Montaigne

seem easy to trust a player like Johnson, but Fitzsimmons did the same things with other clubs and players, like Phil Ford, Otis Birdsong, Randy Smith, Lou Hudson and Pete Maravich.

Today the science of the game is overpowering the art. More things are controlled and calculated. Red Auerbach thought statistics were for losers. Red Holtzman didn't want to call plays because he wanted his guards to understand the flow and feeling of the game and call the plays themselves. He'd say, "I don't care what play you call, just execute it." I hope Fitzsimmons continues to influence Danny Ainge, the Suns and the art of the game.

One of the most dreaded transitions of a professional athlete's life is moving from his or her sport to another endeavor. The NFL Players Association, along with Ball State University, consulted with retired football players and concluded that 65 percent go through emotional problems after leaving the sport. A similar percentage would probably exist in the NBA.

Wayman Tisdale would be an exception. He's had an excellent NBA career and has been affected by his on-the-court environment. But Wayman will likely have less problems after retirement because he has a passion, a talent and developed skills that are separate from the game of basketball. Wayman is an accomplished jazz musician. He can throw himself into his music and the cheering will continue and the adrenaline will still flow. We all need more than one passion.

Cedric Ceballos

"Believe in yourself and your method to achieve your goal. Understand that you are unique and trust your steps to achieve your goal."

"Understand that you are human. There are right things and wrong things that you'll do. Correct the bad and do good. Keep focused and adjust to the positive side of things."

Kevin Johnson
"Understand the fundamentals and continue to want to improve."

"If you want to soar like eagles you must have faith."

Kevin Johnson

"Simplicity, Simplicity. I say let you affairs be as two or three and not a hundred or a thousand, and keep you accounts on your thumbnail.

— Henry David Thoreau

Danny Manning
"Be unselfish. Try to make the game easier for your teammates. Don't worry about things that you can't control."

Jason Kidd
"A family atmosphere is important."

John "Hot Rod" Williams
"Pay attention and always learn. Never talk back to the coach - listen."

"Treat people the way you want to be treated."

Wayman Tisdale
"Try to expand, learn more than basketball and that may also help your basketball. It's all about drive and desire."

"A life is not impor-tant except in the impact it has on other lives.

— Jackie Robinson

"Nothing beats hard work. No one will give you any-thing."

Rex Chapman
"For my whole life I was more talented than my opponent. At this level everybody is talented. So the question now is who works the hardest."

"Nothing worth anything is ever easy. When I was 8 years old, I heard Dr. J say something to that effect. It stayed with me."

Dominant personality
Kevin Johnson

Care-giver
Kevin Johnson

PORTLAND TRAILBLAZERS

T HERE IS A void in Portland. The fans there have had a long-term love affair with their Blazers. They were hooked on high energy, fast-break, championship-caliber basketball. The fans were up close and personal. They energized the team and the team responded. They had confidence in three classy all stars. Terry Porter, Clyde Drexler and Buck Williams. Porter was prepared, focused, and controlled the tempo of the game. Drexler could do everything at a star level and he did it with grace and ease. Williams kept everything *real*. He was strong, physical and played in the trenches.

These players gave them great leadership and took them to two NBA finals. The fans knew what to expect and they appreciated them greatly. At the start of warm-ups, the public address announcer would say "Trailblazers in the house" and everyone would quickly rise to their feet and start clapping. But now all of that has changed. There is a new bigger arena, the Rose Garden. It is harder to sell out. The fans still love them but they don't know exactly what to expect. They seem to want to know how to interpret, or receive, this team. They are looking for players who can connect them to this new team.

Clifford Robinson is the link to the past. He is the only guy remaining from Portland's two appearances in the NBA finals. He is a colorful all-star who can score from the three-point area or on the blocks. He is one of the few players since Wilt Chamberlain to wear headbands. He has a red one, a white one and a black one. One long-time fan would wear the same color headband that Robinson would wear. When Robinson would change, the fan would change. His headbands brought him a little closer to the fans.

Chris Dudley has played solid defense, rebounded well, and blocked shots. He is a deceptive shot blocker as opposed to a challenging one. He doesn't stand in the middle of the lane and take all challenges. Dudley just appears, surprises the opponents and blocks the shot.

He graduated from Yale University with a degree in economics and political science. His parents, grandfather, and uncle attended Yale. His grandfather, Gilford Dudley, served as an ambassador to Denmark under presidents Nixon and Ford. Dudley received the Walter B. Kennedy Citizenship Award in 1996. He donated $300,000 to the Oregon chapter of the I Have a Dream Foundation. He also donated $100,000 to Gales Creek Camp in Oregon.

Kenny Anderson is the player who now runs the show. He left New Jersey as their all-time leader in assists. Anderson was a New York playground legend and the nation's top high school recruit. In two seasons at Georgia Tech, he moved into the school's top five all-time in scoring, assists and steals, and averaged 23 points a game. On offense, Anderson anticipates what could or would happen. Former Hawks center and Orlando assistant coach Tree Rollins has a saying, "You can't teach seven feet." You also can't teach court savvy and anticipation skills. You either have it or you don't. Anderson has it. The Blazers and their fans are going to be all right. _____

"He who would do his job would see that his first lesson is to know what he is and what is proper for him. Wisdom is always content with the present and never displeased with itself."

— Cicero

Rasheed Wallace
"Work as hard as you can when you're on the floor and success will come to you."

"If you work hard and you're honest and you live right success will come to you.

Cliff Robinson
"Always put your best foot forward."

"Stay focused on what you want to get done. Never give up your belief that you can succeed. There will be times when you could have doubts, but stay focused."

"Let me tell you the secret that has led me to my goal. My strength lies solely in my tenacity."

— Louis Pasteur

Cliff Robinson

Chris Dudley

"Always stay with it. I was the classic late bloomer. I played junior varsity my junior year in high school. I did well my senior year. I wasn't highly recruited. I was one of the few Ivy League players to make it. I think staying with it was important."

"Go for your goals. Try to get the most out of life. Don't be afraid to try. even if you fail, you're better off trying. Education was my backup."

> *"I have been blessed with this talent. It was my duty, responsibility to go out there and do something with it."*
>
> — *Michael Johnson*

Kenny Anderson

"The harder you work, the luckier you get. When things aren't going well, get in the gym, work hard and get back on track."

"What we are is God's gift to us, what we become is our gift to him. He gives us talents, we have to take advantage of them to thank him for our gifts."

Isaiah Rider

"Learn how to be consistent. Don't get down when times are tough."

"Stay professional and learn that opinions and impressions are significant in life."

Dominant personality
Cliff Robinson

Care-giver
Chris Dudley

Kenny Anderson

SACRAMENTO KINGS

MAHMOUD ABDUL-RAUF is focused, sincere, and very spiritual. His shooting accuracy, quick release and quick crossover dribble make him a potent offensive weapon. He possibly could have set NCAA scoring records if he had stayed in school for four years. He averaged 30.2 points per game as a freshman and 27.8 points per game as a sophomore. He entered the NBA after only two years of LSU basketball. His shooting accuracy is highlighted by his free throw success. Good jump shooters should be good free-throw shooters. Abdul-Rauf has the second-highest season percentage in league history. He shot 95.6 percent during one season. Only Calvin Murphy shot better with a 95.8 percent rate.

The name Mahmoud Abdul-Rauf means elegant and praiseworthy, servant of the most kind. In speaking with Mahmoud, I developed an appreciation for his commitment. He asked me if I wanted his personal beliefs. When I answered yes, Abdul-Rauf spoke from deep inside his heart. He has had some obstacles to overcome and has done an outstanding job of staying focused. I have great respect for Mahmoud. After all, there is not much more you can ask of a person other than his sincerity and willingness to help people. Abdul-Rauf gives his best.

Olden Polynice shares Abdul-Rauf's strong sense of commitment and purpose. He is a native of Port-au-Prince, Haiti. He once went on a hunger strike to protest America's treatment of Haitian refugees. Olden founded the H.O.O.P. foundation, Helping Out Other People. The organization lends a hand to those less fortunate in the United States and Haiti. He also has a free basketball camp for physically and mentally challenged youth.

Mitch Richmond has a heart of gold and a game to match it. Clyde Drexler once described Richmond as "tough as they come," both offensively and defensively. He is one of the top three shooting guards in the NBA. Richmond is a quiet, classy guy who goes about his job in a subtle way. He also makes big contributions to Daysprings Outreach, a program for troubled youth in the West Sacramento area.

"Prayer is a medium through which I ask God to show me God's will, and to give me strength to carry out that will. God's will alone matters not my personal desires or needs. When I played tennis I never prayed for victory in a match. I will not pray now to be cured of heart disease or AIDS.

— Arthur Ashe

Olden Polynice

"No excuses — just results. We get too wrapped up making excuses rather than producing. Stand up and take responsibility."

"Stay positive and believe in yourself. A lot of people told me I couldn't make it. You can't listen to doubters or people getting in your business."

Tyus Edney

"You should always be able to look in the mirror after a game or practice and know that you've done your best."

"Always be positive and keep the Lord first."

Bobby Hurley

"For a small player, you have to know what to practice. You have to spend a lot of time."

"Staying close to your family is important."

Lionel Simmons

"The only way to be successful is to work hard and not let obstacles stop you. It won't be easy."

"Never take life for granted whether the going is good or bad. Realize every day is a blessing."

Mitch Richmond
"Be honest with yourself and know what you want out of life. And keep the Lord in your life."

"You commit a sin of omission if you do not utilize all the power that is within you. All men have claims on man, and to the man with special talents, this is a very special claim. It is required that a man take part in the actions and clashes of his time than the peril of being judged not to have lived at all."

— Oliver Wendall Holmes.

Mitch Richmond

Mahmoud Abdul-Rauf

Mahmoud Abdul-Rauf

"Whatever I do, I do for the sake of the Almighty who gave me what I have. Which of the favors of the Lord will you deny? I don't want to waste one second of my time. I want to be appreciative of the gifts. I keep focused that way."

"Don't depend on people to get you going, they will disappoint you."

Dominant Personality
Mitch Richmond

Care Giver
Olden Polynice

SAN ANTONIO SPURS

DOMINIQUE WILKINS MAY be the most underrated superstar in the history of the game. He and Bob McAdoo were the most accomplished players left off the list of the NBA's 50 greatest players. Wilkins is seventh on the all-time scoring list and still going strong after missing one year of NBA action. He played one year in Greece.

There are several reasons he has never received superstar recognition. He played most of his career in Atlanta. The Atlanta fans don't have the passion for basketball nor the star adulation that is common in some NBA cities. Also, he has played on very good teams, but has never gone to the conference finals.

Some people feel that a superstar should be able to carry his team at least that far. Usually it takes three stars or a fantastic team system to win championships. Wilkins has also been unfairly compared to Michael Jordan, Larry Bird, and Magic Johnson. These great players of his prime had exceptional leadership, play-making and scoring abilities. Wilkins first and foremost is a scorer. His greatest assets are his hard work and his charismatic personality. In spite of having to prove himself every step of the way, Wilkins feels satisfied that his peers have recognized his contributions. When Jordan said the fans have never given Wilkins the credit that he deserves, somehow that made everything better for Wilkins.

It was a pleasure talking to David Robinson. I was very interested to hear his keys to success. How could he be so disciplined, dedicated and talented? This "Officer and a Gentleman" proved to be everything to the Spurs. The team fell apart without him. I found it remarkable that he was a math major, a Naval officer, a musician, a spiritual leader and a league MVP. Then I read about his parents and their book, "How to Raise A MVP." Now I understand that his parents are the source of his greatness.

The race is not to the swift, nor the battle to the strong, neither yet bread to the wise, nor yet riches to men of understanding, nor yet favor to men of skill; but time and chance happened to them all.

— Ecclesiastes 9:11

David Robinson

"It's more than going out and playing a game. It is a responsibility. It's fun, but you can affect a lot of lives positively. Trivia questions don't matter. The kind of person you are matters."

"Have as much fun as you can, but always remember the big picture is important."

Chuck Person

"Stay healthy. Keep in good condition; longevity depends on conditioning and that'll also help your athletic ability."

"Be true to yourself."

Avery Johnson

"Stay humble and hungry. The humble part is to recognize that God has blessed you with talent. The hungry part is to remember don't ever be satisfied. If you score 10, look for 20. Never be satisfied."

Sean Elliott

"I used to always think that there is someone out there that is practicing harder and he may be better than me. So I did extra to try to catch up."

"Always treat people the way you want to be treated. It's simple but effective."

Vinny Del Negro

"Jim Valvano used to tell me, 'Everybody is an ordinary person. Try to do something extraordinary, something that no one thinks you can do or accomplish.'"

"Believe in yourself, know what your strengths are. When people said I couldn't, it made me work harder."

Dominique Wilkins
"Self confidence, along with the will and the determination, make you successful. You have to make sacrifices to be your best."

"Enjoy life. You only live once. You can't be uptight and stressed out. A lot of people with money aren't happy. You need peace of mind."

"We are not permitted to choose the frame of our destiny. But what we put into it is ours."

— *Dag Hammarskjold*

Dominique Wilkins

Charles Smith

"Teams that win have a spiritual bond. They may pray before games. A good mesh of people is more important than talent. Good teams have a coach that is willing to listen, not just hear, to all the players."

"No matter what the circumstances, realize there are two sides to every story; learn both sides before you form an opinion."

Vernon Maxwell

"You have to have a strong mind and a strong will. Be mentally prepared to play every night. If you don't you can get busted."

"It is important to take care of your family. Spend time with them and help to prepare them. My goal is to see my children become successful."

Unto whomsoever much is given, of him shall much be required.

— Luke 12:48

Dominant Personality
David Robinson

Caregiver
Avery Johnson

David Robinson

SEATTLE SUPERSONICS

P ART OF THE strength of the Sonics is their pressing, trapping defense. Their "D" has been called a form of "organized chaos." You have to watch closely to appreciate key components of their success. In any chaos you might assume that there is an absence of order. You'd think that maybe they're good by chance. But this is not the case. The Sonics have a couple of outstanding conductors in Gary Payton and Nate McMillan.

They also have several veteran players who are extremely professional and directed. By this I mean they play a definite role, come to work hard every day, sacrifice personal goals for the good of the team, and get along well with coaches and teammates. Hersey Hawkins, Sam Perkins and McMillan are the silent leaders of this group.

First, let's talk about the conductors. Payton entered the NBA from Oregon State University. He seemed overrated and over-confident. He talked too much and was drafted too high. Sure he had great credentials in the Pac-10 Conference. But that conference was no longer as prestigious as it had been. Averaging 26 points per game and shooting over 50 percent were no small feats. His trash-talking helped to propel him to new heights. First of all he had to back up his talk, and secondly it challenged players to play hard against him. By his third year, he began to blossom. He would later become the first guard since Michael Jordan to win the Defensive Player of the Year award. He has also been named to the first team all-defensive team for three years in a row. Now he can read situations on the floor, anticipate events and make a team defense work properly. He missed just two games in his first six years as a pro. Payton's mom once said, "Gary needs to be happy. Being happy and confident are two important things in this league." She's right and Gary is both.

McMillan has played his entire career with the Sonics. No guard plays ten years with one team unless he is intelligent, a team player, respectful and talented. Nate is all of that. players like Nate and Vern Fleming, Eddie Johnson and Ricky Pierce are willing to play in the shadows of other stars. Nate often finished in the top ten in several categories and occasionally he finished first. He has led the NBA in steals. he's finished second in "Sixth Man of the Year" voting and second in steal to turnover ratio. He and Gary Payton say they would pay Tim Hardaway to teach them his crossover dribble.

"For a man to achieve all that is demanded of him he must regard himself as greater than he is."

— Goethe

Hawkins and Perkins are efficient players who are easy to sacrifice some of their potential. Both players are skilled enough to score more points. Hersey led the nation in scoring as a senior (36.3 points per game). He is the fourth all-time leading scorer in NCAA history (3,008 points). He has also only missed seven games in eight years. Sam Perkins played in all 82 games for the third time in his career. "Big Smooth" could start for most NBA clubs. He plays his role and contributes when called upon. Of course the Sonics are very dependent on Shawn Kemp's hard work and skill as well as Detlef Schrempf.

Terry Cummings
"A key is the discipline of consistency. It requires quiet time."

"Put God first as a foundation and build off that."

Nate McMillan
"I tell kids in camp, 'Be the best you can be at whatever you do, then you can never fail as long as you

know you've done your best."

"Spike Lee's movie had the right idea, 'Do the right thing.' Common sense is more important than intelligence."

Gary Payton
"My father told me you have to listen and not be a hard head. Good advice will always come back to help you."

"Work hard and take care of important things like your body and your family."

"If you fix your mind on the goal of winning and stay honest with yourself, you'll come to realize that winning isn't about right and wrong or the good guys and the bad guys or the pathway to good life and character or statistics. Winning is about who has the best team and that's all".

— Bill Russell

Gary Payton

"God has blessed us and we have to give back and advise young people."

Sam Perkins
"Keep your nose clean."

"Take care of the hand that takes care of you."

"Remember people that helped you earlier."

Hersey Hawkins
"Go out and work hard despite what happens."

"After every game and practice, you should be able to look in the mirror and know you've done your best."

"Have a good base and put God first. Faith is important, everything else will fall in place."

Shawn Kemp
"Regardless of what you do, a good work ethic and a sense of direction are important."

"Enjoy yourself. Life should be full of fun and hard work."

Dominant personality
Gary Payton

Care-giver
Nate McMillan

Shawn Kemp

TORONTO RAPTORS

ISAIAH THOMAS HAS cast a very big and positive image on the Raptors' front office. First, he gave them an image of success and a smile. This gives fans something to believe in while the strategies are being formed. He also shared his history of competing and producing winners. Because he had primarily reshaped the destiny of the Pistons, he could show this expansion organization how to compete. In selecting a coach, he wanted one that could lose without becoming a loser. He also provides meals for his team after their shooting practices on the road. I think that is a very good idea and the Raptors are the only team that I've seen have that meal together.

Damon Stoudamire is as quick as any guard in the NBA and has great range for his jump shot. Stoudamire was a controversial pick but a perfect fit for the Raptors. He went on to become the Rookie of the Year. The fans believe Stoudamire will eventually make the Raptors a very good team. He'll help to make his teammates better because he's creative and quick enough to produce easy shots. The Raptors will, however, need another star before they can make a run for the playoffs. Marcus Camby may fill that role if he can remain healthy.

Walt Williams may develop into the additional star that the Raptors need. He continues to improve and focus his work on key aspects of his game. Knowing where to concentrate your efforts can be half of the battle. In college, he was nicknamed "The Wizard" because of his passing and ball handling skills, but he also averaged 26.8 points per game his senior year at the University of Maryland. He ranks in the top 10 in points, assists, steals, field goals made, free throws made, and shots blocked in Sacramento Kings' history. Hard off-season work has given him a much better outside shot. Williams is also liked by his teammates. He wears his socks up to his knees in the style of one of his heroes, George Gervin. After being traded from Sacramento, the Kings' starters in the next game recognized Williams by wearing their socks as high as they could.

————————

"The most important single ingredient in the formula of success is knowing how to get along with people."

— Theodore Roosevelt

Damon Stoudamire
"Always play hard regardless of the outcome."

"Don't get caught up in glamour or fame and take life one day at a time."

Walt Williams
"I wasn't always good. I had to work. I wanted to be one of the best. I knew I had to work."

"Attaining success was my goal. Don't let anything stand in our way. I didn't want to disappoint my parents."

Sharone Wright
"Know what you want and don't get too comfortable."

"The better players always keep working. That's why I always shoot 80 shots before a game to become a better shooter."

Popeye Jones
"Never take anything for granted; work hard for everything."

"Remember basketball is only a game, there is life otherwise."

Damon Stoudamire

"The tragedy in life doesn't lie in not reaching your goal. The tragedy lies in having no goal to reach. It isn't a calamity to die with dreams unfulfilled, but it is certainly a calamity not to dream. It is not a disaster to be unable to capture your ideal, but it is a disaster to have no ideal to capture."

— Dr. Benjamin E. Mays

Dominant personality
Damon Stoudamire

Care-giver
Walt Williams

"In any moment of decision the best thing you can do is the right thing, the next best thing is the wrong thing and the worst thing you can do is nothing."

— Theodore Roosevelt

Marcus Camby

UTAH JAZZ

THE JAZZ ARE built around John Stockton and Karl Malone. They've only missed four games each throughout their NBA career. The consistency of their effort has yielded the consistency of their results.

Stockton is very deceptive. Gary Payton calls him "tricky." He has a timid appearance and the discipline of players from an older generation. He doesn't wear long uniform shorts and his shirttail is always in his pants. In reality, Stockton is very physical, competitive and aggressive. He reads defenses as well as anyone in the NBA. He executes the pick and roll so well because he always takes what the defense gives. Early in Stockton's career, he played the vice president of public relations, David Allred, in a friendly game to pass the time. Stockton spotted Allred 20 points in a game to 22. Allred never touched the ball, as Stockton scored 22 straight points.

His mentality is not uncommon among outstanding athletes. Lou Hudson believed that he should shoot the ball more than anyone else on the team. Hudson believed that he was the best shooter and therefore should take the most shots whether he was playing recreational ball, two-on-two, or the NBA All-Star Game.

The essence of basketball is twofold. It is rhythm and position. Malone may be the greatest offensive position player in the history of the game. He doesn't possess great fluid rhythmic moves, but he gets remarkable position around the basket. The defense then must foul him and/or give him an easy basket. Sometimes people overlook Malone's effectiveness because he scores often from the free-throw line. He has a reciprocal relationship with the fans. They like to be recognized by Malone as much as he likes their applause. He raises his hands like a musical conductor and the crowd responds with applause and smiles of appreciation.

Karl Malone
"Give everything you have to the game and the fans."

Have regard for your name, since it will remain for you longer that a great store of gold.

Ecclesiastes 42:12

"Learn to appreciate and respect the game and life."

John Stockton
"Stay willing to learn and listen."

"Leave yourself as many options as possible."

Jeff Hornacek
"Play hard and always give your best."

"Keep out of trouble."

Antoine Carr
"You can always learn more."

"Hard work and good friends are a big part of any success."

Chris Morris
"You have to have fun. It can keep you renewed."

"Family can keep you going in hard times."

John Stockton

"In sports, it isn't hard to be good from time to time. What's tough is being good every day."

— *Willie Mays*

Dominant personality
Karl Malone

Care-giver
John Stockton

Karl Malone & John Stockton

VANCOUVER GRIZZLIES

FOR 17 YEARS, I've conducted a nonprofit basketball camp for deaf athletes. Ninety percent of the participants are hearing-impaired and 10 percent can hear and talk. Shareef Abdur-Rahim, now playing for Vancouver, was recommended for the camp because he was a solid citizen, a good player, and a very good friend of Vernon Jennings, a hearing player who had participated in the camp before. Jennings' mother and sisters had helped me tremendously with the camp over the years. There was one problem. Abdur-Rahim, after his junior year in high school, was already the number one player in Georgia. We had some very good players from New Jersey and Washington, D.C., but none good enough to play on Abdur-Rahim's level. He agreed to volunteer at the camp instead. He played one-on-one, coached, offered counseling, kept score and even helped clean.

Hearing-impaired youngsters have a unique sense of knowing whether someone is genuine. They watch how the person interacts and communicates. All of my kids loved Shareef and still follow and applaud his success.

Abdur-Rahim grew up in the Atlanta area as a big fan of Dominique Wilkins. Role models are very important to young aspiring athletes. Watching these models gives inspiration, dreams and a focus. Kids play countless imaginary games with and against them. They also see themselves responding to game situations as their heroes do. As the young players become pros, they are usually carriers of some trace characteristics of their heroes. Sometimes you have to look closely or know who the heroes are to recognize the similarity.

Abdur-Rahim had the opportunity to play against and impress Wilkins. He said, "When I was a kid, he was my favorite player in the world. I was a Dominique fan. I had the jersey, the autograph and the hair cut."

Abdur-Rahim had 18 points, nine rebounds, nine assists and only one turnover against Wilkins and his Spurs. Wilkins had 26 points, 11 rebounds and one turnover. Wilkins had praise for his young admirer after the game. "What I like about guys like him is that they've got some heart," he said. "He plays hard. And I respect a kid like that, who comes out and gives it his all. A young guy who accepts the challenge. You don't see a lot of young guys do that. He's going to be a great one."

Maybe Wilkins was praising Abdur-Rahim for the qualities he saw in himself. Regardless, Abdur-Rahim will treasure Wilkins' assessment for life.

"It is our duty to conserve our physical powers, our intellectual endowments, our spiritual ideals.

—W. E. B. DuBois

Blue Edwards

"The biggest thing is a sense of discipline. There are rules and regulations you must follow to play a game and live in society. Be patient and strive to be better without stepping on other people."

"Listen and think. A lot of people can give you advice. Before you take action, think of consequences and benefits. It seems like a lot but it only takes two or three seconds."

Greg Anthony

"Good things happen to those who prepare for it. And the only way to prepare for it is hard work. When no one else is practicing, you practice. When someone else is working, you work harder. If you do that you will be rewarded in ways that you never imagined."

George Lynch

"Never stop dreaming. Never stop believing in yourself."

Anthony Peeler

"Have fun at whatever you do. Think of basketball as an activity and not an everyday thing in our life."

Shareef Abdur-Rahim

"Continue to get better. Being young, I look at great players and try to see what made them great. They all improved from year to year."

"Make good decisions. The values and structure of your life are important."

"Keep a good balance and stay around good people. Good people do good things."

Shareef Abdur-Rahim

"You are the way and the wayfarers. And when one of you falls down he falls for those behind him, a caution against the stumbling stone. Ay, and he falls for those ahead of him, who though faster and surer of foot, yet removed not the stumbling stone."

— Kahlil Gibran

Bryant "Big Country" Reeves
"Be happy on the floor and enjoy what you're doing. Know that you're doing the best you can."

"You must be as good a person as you can be. Be satisfied with yourself. What you do reflects on who you are."

Dominant personality
Shareef Abdur-Rahim

Care-giver
Blue Edwards

Greg Anthony & Bryant Reeves

WASHINGTON BULLETS

WES UNSELD HAS quietly been a very positive influence on the Bullets organization since 1968. He came into the league with a bang. He was NBA Rookie of the Year and the league's Most Valuable Player. He and Wilt Chamberlain are the only two players to win both awards in one year. Even though Unseld was a great force in helping to send the Bullets to 12 consecutive playoff appearances and a world championship in 1978, he has been satisfied to play in the shadows. His former teammate and a fantastic player in his own right, Elvin Hayes, got most of the publicity and attention. Wes went on to win the NBA's first Walter B. Kennedy Citizenship Award and he and his wife, Connie, started the Unseld School just outside Baltimore. Today, the school serves 200 students in preschool through fifth grade, with a student teacher ratio of 12-1. Sometimes if you are quiet and not self-promoting, the lessons that you have to teach are not heard.

Recently, a former student at Morehouse College told me that he was in school while Dr. Benjamin E. Mays was president of the college. He said he never realized until years later that Mays was such an outstanding person with so many lessons to teach. He never knew that Mays had been an early mentor to the Rev. Martin Luther King Jr. Nor did he know that Mays had been advisor to John F. Kennedy and Lyndon Johnson. Mays also visited and discussed non-violent resistance with India's Mohandas Gandhi in 1936. Along with his 49 honorary degrees, Mays was internationally respected as one of the most celebrated educators and orators of the 20th century. His influence was felt but not fully appreciated. Mays was not a self-promoter. In fact, he often quoted and seemed to live by the words of the prophet Micah "He has showed you, o man, what is good, and what does the Lord require of you but to do justice and to love kindness, and to walk humbly with your God?" As Bishop Earl Paulk of Chapel Hill Harvester Church in Decatur, Georgia, has said, "That was your free part."

The Bullets should listen attentively to Wes Unseld.

Washington's hope for the future is built around two talented and intelligent young front court players. Chris Webber and Juwan Howard are excellent candidates to learn from their predecessors, Unseld and Hayes. Howard credits his grandmother with instilling in him the values that have made him successful. She passed away after Howard signed his letter of intent at Michigan.

Webber has a touch of flash in his game. And through all the injuries and coaching changes, he has managed to register several triple doubles. Webber has an extensive collection of signed historical documents of prominent African-Americans, including items from the Rev. Dr. Martin Luther King, Jr. and Frederick Douglass.

As I hear more from Webber, my respect for him grows. I like the fact that he represents himself and others well. He also has respect for players who paved the way for today's athletes. He said that during a hard time in his career, Bill Russell offered a kind statement. It was a simple word of encouragement. Russell said, "I like what you guys are doing." Because of Webber's respect for Bill Russell, that positive comment remained with him all year and inspired him to try harder.

"Cultivate the tree which you have found to bear fruit in your soil. Regard not your past failures or success. All the past is equally a failure and a success. It is a success in as much as it offers you the present opportunity."

— Henry David Thoreau

Chris Webber
"Without hard work nothing gets accomplished."

"In the midst of turmoil, remember who you are."

"The people in the church did not contribute one dime to help me with my education. But they gave me something far more valuable. They gave me encouragement.

-Dr. Benjamin E. Mays

Chris Webber

Gheorghe Muresan
"You need work with height also. No one gives you anything free."

"Get a good education and find what you want out of life."

Calbert Cheaney
"Hard work and determination and having people believe in me and not give up helped me to get here."

"My mom taught me to trust your friends and not your buddies."

Rod Strickland
"Confidence is the biggest part. Then persistence and hard work are next. You have to be mentally tough."

Harvey Grant
"Go out and give 110 percent. If you win, you win. If you lose, you lose. You can look at yourself in the mirror and say you've done your best. And you get the respect of your peers."

"First respect yourself and then treat other people with respect."

Juwan Howard
"With your dreams, you have to work hard to have success."

Dominant personality
Chris Webber

Care-giver
Juwan Howard

"I thank God for my handicaps for through them, I have found myself, my work and my God."

-Helen Keller

Juwan Howard

Thank you for caring enough about my opinion to read this book. Allow me to share the thoughts of one more outstanding individual. Earl Manigault was one of the biggest playground legends in New York City's history. He made some unfortunate decisions that prevented him from playing NBA basketball. Nontheless, "The Goat," as he was called, is still respected as a star of the game of basketball. There was even a television movie, "Rebound," about his life. Manigault now works hard to keep young people in New York working toward their goals. I asked him about his basketball experience.

"I wasn't afraid to try new things," Manigault said, "things that I had never seen done before."

I then asked him if he felt cheated because he never got a chance to show his talents to the nation. His response, "I wasn't cheated by anyone else. I was cheated by myself."

It was a pleasure to share the thoughts that help to create the successes of the people featured in this book. I hope that you will be inspired to better define success for your life. And in your creative journey to achieve that success, I trust you'll never cheat yourself.

Mike "Stinger" Glenn

Photographers Credits

Photographers names are listed in order of appearance.

Scott Cunningham	Bill Baptist
Chris Covatta	Noren Trotman
Nathaniel S. Butler	Glenn James
Fernado Medina	Noren Trotman
Bill Baptist	Nathaniel S. Butler
Nathaniel S. Butler	Nathaniel S. Butler
Scott Cunningham	Noren Trotman
Scott Cunningham	Fernando Medina
Doug DeVoe	Bill Baptist
Tim Defrisco	Sandy Tenuto
Layne Murdoch	Andrew D. Bernstein
Glenn James	Steve DiPaola
Scott Cunningham	Chris Covatta
Andy Hayt	Sam Forencich
Sam Forencich	Ray Amati
Chis Covatta	D. Clarke Evans
Sam Forencich	Andrew D. Bernstein
Barry Gossage	Andrew D. Bernstein
Andrew D. Bernstein	Noren Trotman
Glenn James	Jerry Wachter
Chris Covatta	Barry Gossage
Andrew D. Bernstein	Sam Forncich
Chris Corvatta	Christopher J. Relke
Andrew D. Bernstein	Andrew D. Bernstein
Andrew D. Bernstein	Sam Forencich
Andrew D. Bernstein	Scott Cunningham
Richard Lewis	Marvin Scott

Michael, Rhonda, and Michael Justin Glenn

AUTOGRAPHS

AUTOGRAPHS

AUTOGRAPHS